Is Atheism a Theism?
and other essays

The Unnecessary Conflict

Is Atheism a Theism?

and other essays

The Unnecessary Conflict

Ronald Ford

GEORGE RONALD

OXFORD

George Ronald, Publisher
Oxford
www.grbooks.com

*A catalogue record for this book is available
from the British Library*

ISBN 978–0–85398 580–8

Cover design: Steiner Graphics

CONTENTS

'The harmony of religious belief with reason is a new vista which Bahá'u'lláh has opened for the soul of man.'

'Abdu'l-Bahá

Foreword

by Professor Suheil Bushrui

Many of the voices broadcasting today on religion and atheism contribute to divisiveness and fragmentation, a state of affairs fuelled by a media obsessed with sensationalism and controversy. The result is that an impassioned dialectic of extremes pits fanatical religious rhetoric against an arrogant and narrow-minded rationality devoid of soul. It is time to offer an alternative vision – one that recognizes the precious integrity, value and validity of religion and the religious experience.

In this tense and polarized environment, it is undoubtedly challenging for the honest seeker to find a sober perspective on the role of religious experience in human life. Religion serves in part to keep us aware of that mystery which is the 'ultimate reality'. This awareness engenders a sense of worship, of submission, of sanctity and holiness. It is, however, a lack of appreciation for mystery, awe, and wonder that separates the New Atheists from those scientists and investigators of the past who were endowed with vision and a full realization of the limitations of the human mind. Indeed, the recognition of the mystery at the heart of reality is, in fact, neither ignorance nor wishful thinking, but rather a form of wisdom higher than ordinary knowledge.

The New Atheists do not represent a new phenomenon; one finds systematic and organized rejections of both metaphysics and religious values even before the time of Christ. The Cyrenaic school of Ancient Greece and the Carvakas

of ancient India, for example, proposed materialistic philosophies, denying reality and worth to anything beyond the
physical senses. Variations on such perspectives – whether they
are called hedonism, nihilism, materialism or scientism – rear
their head in every age, under different names and in different
conditions. Today's atheism differs little from the reductionist
arguments and anti-religious sentiment of the nineteenth and
twentieth centuries.

In their critique, the New Atheists have completely forgot-
ten to consider the noble and enlightening aspect of religion
with its philosophical, mystical, experimental and practical
dimensions, and have opted instead in favour of a straw-man
depiction of religion that is easily refuted. There is no denying
that literalism and the use of religion to achieve political ends
has shackled the spirit of some forms of modern religiosity.
This kind of literalistic approach and the politicization of religion seems to dominate the New Atheist critique. All that is
well and good for philosophical rumination – and individuals
such as Richard Dawkins, Sam Harris, Christopher Hitchens
and Daniel Dennet, among others, are entitled to their investigations and speculations – but what is not well and good
is how these ideas are presented as fact and final, remarkably
similar to how religious extremists proclaim their views. What
plagues this type of speculative science is the conceit with
which it is asserted and how differing viewpoints are haughtily
discarded. From their viewpoint, material reality is the only
reality; the final assumption is that the only means to acquire
knowledge is exclusively within the disciplines of the natural
and social sciences. Realities not controllable or measurable
are marginalized, ignored and finally dismissed.

What no materialistic theory is capable of doing, however,
is to offer any meaningful answer to the question why – why
anything exists at all. Even a complete description of how the
physical universe is constituted or how it changes over time
would not diminish its mystery. In a sense, the increase of

empirical knowledge brought about by scientific investigation serves only to amplify our wonder. The sheer immensity of the cosmos and the stunning order manifest in the cycles of nature have been enduring sources of astonishment, forever giving rise to new questions to consider and new beauties to behold. It was Albert Einstein, the most renowned scientist of the twentieth century, who noted that true knowledge is rooted in an awareness of something we cannot penetrate. He writes:

> The most beautiful thing we can express is the mysterious. It is the source of all true art and science. He, to whom this emotion is a stranger, who can no longer pause to wonder and stand apart in awe, is as good as dead: his eyes are closed. This insight into the mystery of life, coupled though it be with fear, has also given rise to religion. To know that what is impenetrable to us really exists, manifesting itself as the highest wisdom and the most radiant beauty which our dull faculties can comprehend only in their most primitive forms – this knowledge, this feeling is at the centre of true religiousness. In this sense, and in this sense alone, I belong in the ranks of devotedly religious men.
>
> The cosmic religious experience is the strongest and noblest driving force behind scientific research. It is enough for me to contemplate the mystery of conscious life perpetuating itself through all eternity, to reflect upon the marvellous structure of the universe which we can daily perceive, to try humbly to comprehend even an infinitesimal part of the intelligence manifested in nature.[1]

In the final analysis, intellectuals such as Einstein, Spinoza and Shelley, who are often included in the pantheon of neo-atheists, may have disagreed with certain theological creeds and the uses to which these were sometimes put. However, unlike today's New Atheists, they did not deny the fundamentally spiritual foundation of reality, but upheld the primacy of the divine, under whatever terminology, as the centre and source of all things.

The New Atheists are, however, not solely to blame for the rampant spiritual illiteracy they demonstrate, nor for their virulent onslaught against the sacred. In large part, the desecration of the temple has been carried out by profit-driven industry and media, especially in television, cinema and art. Such depictions, whether of Jesus, Muhammad, or any other Prophet of God, are unacceptable even from the point of view of good manners; equally intolerable, however, is to compromise one's own moral ground by responding to vulgarity with violent protest.

In order to ensure that the future of humanity is not a bleak dystopia, a spiritual renaissance must engulf the world. For as humanity transitions to a global society the likes of which have never been seen before, the temporal order must come into closer alignment with that of the eternal, divine order – that centre which holds all things together. In each civilization, there is a period of flourishing animated by the distilled spiritual impulse of revelation. From this repository of divine guidance issue forth the means and methods of moral training, education, arts, sciences and philosophy. In other words, it is the very nature of religion to transform not only the fabric of social structures but the categories of human consciousness and civilization as a whole.

As we continue to propose and debate answers to the great questions that define our humanity, we will be encouraging a renewal of all those values that are essential in establishing and maintaining civilized society. The challenge that faces our world today is how to promote conditions in which peoples of faith, as well as those of an atheistic persuasion, can truly work together in harmony.

Suheil Bushrui, Professor Emeritus
College of Behavioral and Social Sciences
University of Maryland

Preface

Faith is the great cop-out, the great excuse to evade the need to think and evaluate evidence.   Richard Dawkins

As the author of this book I have to declare my position. I believe in an omnipotent, unknowable God, or Creator, and I disagree with the claim by Richard Dawkins, quoted above, that faith is a cop-out. Certainly, some religious extremists are intolerant and have interpretations of scripture and science that border upon superstition, but to label faith in its entirety as a 'cop-out' is an insult that is made in order to cause a distraction, a 'provocation'. Dawkins' view, if put more kindly, is that in one sense it should be within the realm of science (or philosophy) to solve any religious dilemma that clashes with science. However, scientists cannot easily absolve themselves from moral dilemmas that may arise from their experiments.

I also resent the constant attacks made upon religion by writers such as Dawkins who tend to avoid discussion based upon mutual respect. The subtitle of this book, *The Unnecessary Conflict*, was chosen because I feel that a shift in the basic current stand-off between atheists and theists would allow each to discover, without verbal conflict, what it is that really divides them and creates such bitterness, and would perhaps empower them to reach a new level of understanding and mutual respect. This book will also attempt to cut through the 'jargon jungle' that permeates and distorts what is an unnecessary conflict between those who choose to believe in a God or Creator and those who reject such beliefs. It will also attempt to examine the mental struggle of many sincere seekers who are trying to rationalize their convictions in this scientific age and thus highlight the fact that there is an urgent need for dialogue between religion and science.

Many of the quotations in this book draw on the writings of the Bahá'í Faith, and particularly of 'Abdu'l-Bahá, one of the Faith's central figures, who in many of his writings and public speeches elaborated on the Bahá'í principle of harmony between religion and science and the necessity of investigating reality with an open mind.

Is Atheism a Theism?

The title of this essay is of course a play on words. Atheists very often focus their attacks on religion upon the traditions, rituals and folklore that have accrued throughout history and tend to avoid the real issue of faith that has sustained and guided humanity onward and upward. The intensity of their crusade is often reminiscent of religious fanaticism, as they claim to seek truth, but truth as they perceive it, and they have complete faith in their convictions. Atheists can therefore sometimes come across as turning their own non-belief into a belief as strong as theism, as is often pointed out about Richard Dawkins, perhaps the most vociferous of the New Atheists: 'He's a believer too – in his own mythology.'[1] At such times the atheistic claim to disbelieve sounds a bit hollow.

In the sense that it is extremely determined to 'prove' that there is no God, atheism – particularly in its incarnation as 'New Atheism' – is a belief that is as strong and vociferous as theism. Atheism and theism are therefore often portrayed as opposing philosophies or belief systems, whereas an agnostic is one who is doubtful – and this is probably a more honest position than rejecting God completely. There is a need to highlight the emptiness of atheism and put the case that religion has a positive role to play in people's lives.

In a way, both atheism and theism are prone to error, for the simple reason that 'existence' or 'non-existence' cannot really be applied to God. Such a Being is beyond human experience, as 'Abdu'l-Bahá writes:

Existence is of two kinds: one is the existence of God which is beyond the comprehension of man. He, the invisible, the lofty and the incomprehensible, is preceded by no cause but rather is the Originator of the cause of causes. He, the Ancient, hath had no beginning and is the all-independent. The second kind of existence is the human existence. It is a common existence, comprehensible to the human mind, is not ancient, is dependent and hath a cause to it. The mortal substance does not become eternal and vice-versa; the human kind does not become a Creator and vice-versa. The transformation of the innate substance is impossible.[2]

The criticisms against religious belief being made today by many intelligent scientists and laymen who claim to be atheist are often prejudiced or biased in a way that borders upon the insolent, insofar as they attack what may be termed the 'underbelly' of religion, such as the myths and stories, rather than conducting a serious analysis of what has really inspired people for thousands of years. I suppose that this negativity is to be expected, given that much of the religious education we have received has centred upon the myths that abound in the popular histories of religious institutions rather than intensive study of the insightful gems of divine mystery that have inspired musicians, poets, artists and writers. In the words of Pablo Picasso (1881–1973): 'The business of an artist is to find where God is hiding.'

The colourful and often pious accounts of religious history that have inspired millions for generations, and sustained the millions who have suffered some form of loss and despair since the dawn of time, arose because the large majority were unable to read and so were not able to study the scriptures (such as were available). People therefore relied upon the stories and legends that were passed on to them to keep their faith alive; these stories enabled them to celebrate and feel happy or reflective at important commemorations and festivals. Sometimes such legends may have been symbolic references that had become distorted over time, but they were part and parcel of the human need to remember and rejoice over significant events of their spiritual heritage. Important events were also symbolized in magnificent works of art and the building of awe-inspiring places of worship. They have all attempted to embody the joy that comes with a creative act and pious belief.

In this age we have more opportunity to study religion in depth and many have come to realize that despite the zealous observance of the celebrations and traditions by the generality of people as being the recognizable face of their religion, because of the ancient roots of these religions there are many inaccuracies in what they believe. Yet we are still able to recognize the core message that has always been one of hope and certitude and vital to the spiritual evolution of the human race at different points in history. We must also accept that the use of ritual is not confined to religion: science, politics and society in general also display a penchant for ritual.

Consider the following, which is known as the atheist paradox and should be disposed of immediately. It goes as follows.

(1) If God exists then he is omniscient, omnipotent and perfectly good.

(2) If God were omniscient, omnipotent and perfectly good then the world would not contain evil.

(3) The world contains evil.

Therefore:

(4) It is not the case that God exists.

Of course, in reality this is not a paradox but a deliberate misconception about the existence or non-existence of a deity, using physical terminology. Such terms do not apply to a spiritual being. The real answer to point three is that evil is the absence of good, just as darkness is the absence of light, and is in no way connected with the existence of God. Instead, evil equates with a *denial* of what is good, and has many causes. This is enlarged upon by Udo Schaefer in the following passage:

> Evil is simply the absence of good, as darkness is the absence of light, ignorance the lack of knowledge, illness the lack of health, weakness the lack of strength, poverty the lack of riches. Therefore all evil can be overcome by the good as can darkness by light, because evil, like darkness, is essentially non-existent. The question arises as to why the divine God, who can never want or approve evil, nevertheless allows it, why he does not prevent man from doing evil – and with it comes the question of suffering in the world. Insofar as people in our time think about religious questions at all, the suffering in the world is the subject which moves them most . . . especially the suffering of the innocent – the question of theodicy – has become the chief objection to the belief in God in our time . . . 'Why do I suffer? That is the rock of atheism . . .'[3]

Controversies over atheism and theism frequently occur in scientific circles and have also caused disagreement as to what should be taught in schools. For many reasons, science education in schools, (despite the efforts of Sacre in the United Kingdom and other government bodies), is constantly sidelining religious education in the drive for exam results and material progress. A major cause of this is the battle for funds that schools and universities have to deal with.

Material progress generally and science in particular are essential for the well-being and progress of humanity, and many scientists endeavour to carry out their work with humility; utilizing their efforts to improve our lives and at the same time attempting to align their research in harmony with ethics and recognized value systems. However, under the influence of atheistic and humanist propaganda, science and religion have become a battleground for hearts and minds.

Herbert Dingle (1894–1978) was not an atheist but an outspoken president of the Royal Astronomical Society who is well known for having had problems with Einstein's Special Theory of Relativity because (he said) it relied entirely on theoretical concepts, not experimental verification. He caused quite a stir with several papers that he produced giving his reasons, and to this day he has his supporters, but those who opposed him said that he had not fully understood the theory. Dingle's original claim that there is an insuperable barrier between science and ethics is also disputable; there should never be a barrier or a battle between science and ethics, because all civilization is ultimately defined and judged by its values or turpitudes. However, he hinted that agreement might be possible, and writing later of this possibility of common agreement between religion and science if they could be satisfactorily defined, he stated:

> Science offers, perhaps, no insuperable difficulty, though our ideas of it have been clarified considerably in the last generation, and the definition now regarded as most satisfactory would scarcely have been suggested at all in the last century. But how can we define religion? . . . the differences are innumerable, and they are fundamental.[4]

Ethics may be defined as the principles of right and wrong that are accepted by an individual or a social group. Scientists cannot opt out of their responsibilities toward society: Einstein was not happy about atomic weapons, Oppenheimer was equally disturbed about the H-bomb and many today are extremely concerned about chemical weapons. Of course there is always potential for disagreement, because of the challenges that beset scientists and inventors. For example, there is often a fight for recognition, pressure from governments, requests for funding, and the possibility of replication of one's research after years of work. Many discoveries are made almost simultaneously and this may also cause much bitterness, especially after decades of research. Then there are the philosophical arguments concerning values and ethics for all of us, that often crop up when the results of experiments and technology are thrust into the spotlight.

> Fifty-eight values including honesty and equality have been found to underpin our attitudes and motivate our decisions. Further, numerous authors have suggested that environmental, economic and social problems currently challenging the world can be addressed by focusing on values and by looking at the way in which individuals see themselves as global citizens. [5]

We now seem to have become entrenched in two opposing camps – those who decry any form of belief in a Creator and those who cling equally tenaciously to an unknowable God who created the universe. In this age we can accept the premise of an unknowable Being while perhaps in the past we could not, but both sides should accept that we can only think in human terms and that this is our weakness.

In a way, then, atheism has itself become a pseudo-religious doctrine using an interpretation of evolution as its scripture and creating a division between believers and non-believers that in the long run is both untenable and unnecessary. There are now almost as many variations of atheism as there are religious sects. Then, in 2004 we saw the appearance of 'New Atheism',[6] which argued for religious doctrines to be countered more forcefully. It is obvious then that atheism has created a divide between believers and non-believers and a tolerant response to intolerant accusations is urgently required.

Leaving aside those who believe that the universe was created just a few thousand years ago (referred to as Creationists), the vast majority of the human race has a realistic understanding that humanity is very ancient and that it is not irrational to believe in God and evolution working in harmony, despite the clamour and derision from those who think otherwise. A true understanding of the process of evolution does not and should not undermine religious faith in a Creator, especially as science is still struggling to explain fully how the inanimate can become animate and some palaeontologists are desperately trying to find the 'missing link' that would confirm their own view of an evolution that would not require divine intervention. We are able to observe the process of evolutionary change over a long period of time from the evidence of fossils but seldom, if ever, do we find the precise point where such change to a *spiritual being* originated – a chicken and egg situation that leads to much debate. A common sense view that is held by followers of the Bahá'í Faith, Islam, and some Christians and Jews, is that Adam was the first Prophet but not the first human being – in effect, the first in this historical cycle to teach that there is a spiritual part of the human psyche that would eventually unfold and become apparent if we paid heed to the teachings that each Prophet would reveal at the appropriate time throughout history. Right or wrong, it is a view that makes sense.

While atheists make full use of extravagant exaggeration to prove their point in their battle with theists, and appear not to be interested in seeking common ground, it is surely just as difficult to 'prove' that there is no Creator as it is to prove that there is. There are however, a plethora of signs and evidence that point to the existence of a God or Creator if you are not in denial and are willing to consider all evidence and arguments without bias. It can also be claimed that atheism is a negative way of thinking that thrives as a system in denial of ultimate reality.

Too often, the oppressive power of religious authority has suppressed questions that went against orthodox belief (for example, the doctrine of infallibility is not to be found in the New Testament); but likewise, some scientific circles have in the past attempted to suppress ideas that have challenged accepted wisdom and by doing so, held up progress.[7]

Intelligent design is another idea, introduced in the United States by creation theorists who claim that it is superior to Darwin's Theory of Evolution in explaining the purpose of life on earth. It is used in attempts to get Darwin's Theory banned from the school curriculum, arguing that the exponents of the Theory do not provide sound scientific proof. They fail to realize or accept that 'intelligent design' does not match the crucial evidence that evolution has been long and gradual. Whilst it is surely logical to accept that there is a Cause or Creator that we cannot fully comprehend or articulate, it is plainly wrong to link this with the suggestion that the time scale of approximately six thousand years is realistic. The growth of knowledge on the subject has been a gradual process.

> There was no magic moment when, on the tree of human evolution, our progenitors were given the keys to the kingdom of knowledge. Intelligence has not been perfected into some state of grace. It is the result of feedback and the totality of effects, the choices made by, and the constraints imposed on, individual experience and on our ancestors, in humanity's quest for survival at every stage of development.[8]

The year 2009 saw the discovery of a new fossil that pushed back the origins of man (in this case a woman who was promptly named Ardi). She had apparently been buried with a large number of her kin and has 'leapfrogged' Lucy (discovered in Ethiopia in 1974) in age. Ardi was also from Ethiopia, although she was found quite a distance away geographically.

Details of this discovery were finally published in October 2009. More recently, in 2013, the discovery in China of a well-preserved fossil has reopened the debate about a 'missing link'. The excitement generated by these discoveries reaches across several areas of study because of the desire to pinpoint, if at all possible, the moment at which our earliest ancestors became a distinct species.

Those against evolution are also concerned about the suggestion that we may be descended from apes, but what Darwinists are really saying is that there may have been a common ancestor and modern apes are but a branch. Nevertheless, there is a uniqueness about humanity that has made us distinct from all other life forms, and I believe that there will never be a 'missing link' found to contradict this. But one good thing about the theory of evolution is that we can now see even more clearly that there is a purpose behind the process and that some great force instigated it. It is life's great journey.

However, a big problem is that religious leaders or 'experts' (in both religion and evolutionary theory) have often deliberately tinkered with the evidence so as to retain control of their sphere of influence. As an example of scientific 'tinkering', evolutionary purists clung tenaciously to 'Piltdown man' from 1912 to 1953 as evidence of the 'missing link' until it was found to have been an elaborate hoax, created by Charles Dawson, an amateur archaeologist.

Belief in a first Cause or God, however primitive the thoughts that went with it, has generated religious movements since humanity was first able to form social units. Philip Allott points out the connection between religion and society:

Among all the processes of social reality-forming, it has been **religion**, which, throughout all the recorded history of human socialising, has had the most powerful effects on individual and social consciousness, and on the practical products of that consciousness. Religion seeks to integrate all value with all reality. Religion seeks to connect an order of the whole universe with the willing and acting of the individual human being . . . So it is that religion is liable to dominate all the willing and acting life of individuals and whole societies.[9]

Although the concepts and ideas that go with religious thought have been questioned by philosophers since ancient Greece (Epicurus), atheism as a recognized movement in opposition to religious doctrines did not appear until the 18th century. It has been mainly concerned with providing a different approach to reasons for our existence and finding logical reasons for not believing in a god or religion. In the battle of words that has resulted, religion has been accused of using brainwashing techniques, because the teaching of religion is made from the earliest age at which the young can comprehend, although this is something at which political movements have also been especially adept under totalitarian regimes.

As we have seen, religion has always tried to portray historical events in stories and parables; a very ancient way of communicating with those who were not able to read and write. Atheists delight in portraying such stories as dangerous myths and religious extremists fall into the trap of clinging to the imagery and thereby losing sight of the real meaning. This is a prime reason why atheists feel that they have to campaign against religious belief, because they perceive the damage to young minds that may be caused by extremism. However, sensible religious people are fully aware of the harm that can be caused by the propagation of false doctrines. Yet atheistic political ideologies pose an even greater danger – where is the atheistic State that has not brought immense suffering on its citizens?

Few publishing seasons pass that do not offer the educated reader a range of new and imaginative analyses of the character of some of the monstrous figures who, during the twentieth century, systematically tortured, degraded and exterminated millions of their fellow human beings. One is invited by scholarly authority to ponder the weight that should be given, variously, to paternal abuse, social rejection, professional disappointments, poverty, injustice, war experiences, possible genetic impairment, nihilistic literature – or various combinations of the foregoing – in seeking to understand the obsessions fuelling an apparently bottomless hatred of humankind. Conspicuously missing from such contemporary speculation is what experienced commentators, even as recently as a century ago, would have recognized as spiritual disease, whatever its accompanying features.[10]

There has also been a proliferation of books attacking religion and promoting Darwin's Theory of Evolution as the better explanation for life on earth and the idea of an evolving universe fits well with their reasoning. Amongst these, Richard Dawkins has virtually become a household name as an exponent of evolution and atheism, but one wonders why such an intelligent scientist takes up half of his book *The God Delusion* in dismantling and attacking traditions and stories, cherry-picking religious literature for the most outlandish and incredulous examples of extreme religious beliefs, rather than seeking common ground to understand the mystery of life amidst the colourful panorama of religious thought and teachings.

People love their festivals, mysteries and folklore, but not all take them seriously, and science itself is also riddled with fabulous myths and heresies. Both scientists and religionists should always seek proof so that there can be a true and logical understanding of any concept that is being investigated; this is the way knowledge advances. Sadly, although many scientists do believe in God, many simply cannot come to terms with the idea that a Creator would be unknowable, except perhaps in a limited way through the founders of the religions, or the

Messengers of God (in Bahá'í terminology they are known as 'Manifestations' of God). They therefore target the claims of religious people with accusations of superstition instead of conducting serious research into why religion has been such a binding force and inspiration for millions. There is no real harm in a sincere atheist finding it difficult to believe in a God, but it is becoming clear that it is mainly the images portrayed in religious movements that bother them.

The stupendous vastness and complexity of space is conclusive evidence to many of the *existence* (if such a word can be used) of a supreme Creator. We are faced with the utter impossibility of decoding or understanding such a Being; therefore any name or description is inadequate, although the immensity of space and the sheer diversity of life on earth are surely the signs of a Power that is awesome, unknowable and incomprehensible and conceals the ultimate Creative Force.

While it is obvious that created beings (humanity) cannot possibly comprehend an Uncreated or Creator/God, it should be equally obvious that each Prophet/Founder of a major religion has been like a 'mirror' reflecting the Divinity, and it is through them and their teachings that answers can be found. 'Abdu'l-Bahá is reported to have said,

> A Divine Manifestation is as a mirror reflecting the light of the Sun. The light is the same and yet the mirror is not the Sun. All the Manifestations of God bring the same Light; they only differ in degree, not in reality.[11]

The analogy can also be extended to science.

> Science may be likened to a mirror wherein the images of the mysteries of outer phenomena are reflected. It brings forth and exhibits to us in the arena of knowledge all the product of the past. It links together past and present. The philosophical conclusions of bygone centuries, the teachings of

the Prophets and wisdom of former sages are crystallized and reproduced in the scientific advancement of today. Science is the discoverer of the past. From its premises of past and present we deduce conclusions as to the future. Science is the governor of nature and its mysteries, the one agency by which man explores the institutions of material creation.[12]

To condemn any theory of creation or the existence of God without providing evidence, and attempting to replace it with a theory of evolution that has a distinctly atheistic bias, is in fact unacceptable science.

> The fundamental principles of the Prophets are scientific, but the forms and imitations which have appeared are opposed to science. If religion does not agree with science, it is superstition and ignorance; for God has endowed man with reason in order that he may perceive reality. The foundations of religion are reasonable. God has created us with intelligence to perceive them. If they are opposed to science and reason, how could they be believed and followed?[13]

In 1929, Edwin Hubble announced that almost all galaxies appeared to be moving away from us. In fact, he found that the universe was expanding – with all the galaxies moving away from each other. Using mathematics and theoretical models, astronomers calculated that an expanding universe must have started from an original point; and deduced that approximately 15 billion years ago was the possible starting point. Assuming that these calculations were correct, they then postulated that it all began with the so-called 'Big Bang'. A few, led by Fred Hoyle and others, promoted the idea of a Steady State Theory, but with the discovery of cosmic microwave background radiation, that theory lost support.

The Big Bang theory suggests that in the very first part of that explosion, somehow or other the 'mix' of the chemical reaction caused it to be carbon-based rather than any other. The fact that it was carbon-based and thus allowed life to form became known as the *Anthropic Principle*. It is yet another example that some scientists are not happy with, because it strongly suggests that the Big Bang was 'fine-tuned' or in other words *created*. Because of this, the Anthropic Principle appeals greatly to theists, who feel that together with prophecy and religious teachings that have stood the test of time it undermines the atheistic standpoint.

We should accept, though, that the Big Bang theory still has limitations with regard to the beginning of the universe and that even the age of the earth is still being discussed and argued over. We should perhaps agree to disagree over the many variables and unexplained events about which we can only conjecture, and the fact that there are constantly changing viewpoints based upon constantly emerging information that still has to be agreed upon.

Scientists labour in vain to encapsulate a Creator within their mind-set that demands absolute proof, and so many of them are persuaded that the concept of God is misguided and they look for physical explanations of the beginnings of the observable universe. We may struggle to accept or comprehend that a mere human cannot 'know' (to have knowledge of) God, but we can be 'aware' through religious texts and other spiritual writings, and even through poetry, music, art or the beauty of nature. In dogmatically claiming that there is no God, many scientists and atheists are really just admitting defeat and taking a line of least resistance. It would much more honest to state that they just do not know. Consider this quotation from the writings of Bahá'u'lláh:

The conceptions of the devoutest of mystics, the attainments of the most accomplished amongst men, the highest praise which human tongue or pen can render are all the product of man's finite mind and are conditioned by its limitations. Ten thousand Prophets, each a Moses, are thunderstruck upon the Sinai of their search at His forbidding voice, 'Thou shalt never behold Me!'; whilst a myriad Messengers, each as great as Jesus, stand dismayed upon their heavenly thrones by the interdiction, 'Mine Essence thou shalt never apprehend!'[14]

It surely follows that such a Being could only be known or comprehended even to a limited extent through something that Itself has created (Prophets or Manifestations of God perhaps?) who might then be enabled to guide or to pass on knowledge to humanity in the form of teachings that would nurture us through the various stages of evolution and enlighten us about some of the attributes of God that we could comprehend.

All that man is able to understand are the *attributes* of Divinity, the radiance of which appears and is visible in worlds and souls.[15]

The search for knowledge

The early astronomers considered themselves a little more enlightened than farmers and desert nomads when they realized that a solar calendar was more accurate than the lunar calendar, but this was of little use to the nomads or farmers who only needed to look to the sky and the phases of the moon to tell when a month had gone by, so the lunar calendar made more sense to them. The early followers of Muhammad were nomads, and in the desert the lunar calendar was natural to them; the moon was a fairly reliable aid in that the phases were easy to observe. This is possibly why the lunar calendar was not changed by Muhammad, even though the Egyptians and other settled groups had realized that the solar calendar was more accurate over a long period of time. The general adoption of the solar calendar took time and is still not universally used today.

Our present-day knowledge of the solar system and the immensity of the universe has been reinforced by modern technology; we have got used to receiving amazing pictures from ever more advanced telescopes such as the Hubble. Prior to the invention of the telescope it was 'obvious' to the ordinary observer that the earth was stationary and that the sun revolved around it. Despite the persecution of Galileo (1564–1642) for his 'heresy' in suggesting that the earth revolved around the sun, by the 18th century the orbits of the planets had been calculated and the earth's orbit of the sun was better understood. In that same century, in the writings of Baha'u'llah it was stated that all 'fixed' stars have their own planets. This statement was not fully understood at the time and we are only now beginning to discover that it is very common. The term 'fixed stars' differentiates the stars (such as our sun) from the planets and comets that we can view with our own eyes, which appeared to be 'wandering' through space.

Thou hast, moreover, asked Me concerning the nature of the celestial spheres. To comprehend their nature, it would be necessary to inquire into the meaning of the allusions that have been made in the Books of old to the celestial spheres and the heavens, and to discover the character of their relationship to this physical world, and the influence which they exert upon it. Every heart is filled with wonder at so bewildering a theme, and every mind is perplexed by its mystery. God, alone, can fathom its import. The learned men, that have fixed at several thousand years the life of this earth, have failed, throughout the long period of their observation, to consider either the number or the age of the other planets. Consider, moreover, the manifold divergencies that have resulted from the theories propounded by these men. Know thou that every fixed star hath its own planets, and every planet its own creatures, whose number no man can compute.[16]

There was an early clash between evolutionists and theists, even though neither could define God to the satisfaction of all. Theists have indeed been losing ground to evolutionists and atheists for many years. This may be not such a bad thing in some respects, in that it offers an opportunity to review our limited understanding of a Creator and helps to separate superstition from the core teachings of the importance of love, justice and compassion in religious teachings!

The statement in the Gospels, 'Seek and ye shall find', hints strongly at the many hidden meanings in scripture which are a challenge to atheists and theists alike. In another context it could also mean that there are many challenges for scientists in unlocking the secrets of nature. But as well as looking at the sky, we also need to look within.

Guidelines for ethical behaviour – what should be considered right or wrong – have traditionally been found in the Holy Books of religon, although there is always the possibility that in the older works there is a higher chance of error in interpreting the meanings (because the original works no longer exist) and circumstances in human society change and evolve. Religion is not exclusively for individuals; it is for society and affects progress. Then again, an action that would have been considered sinful two or three thousand years ago may no longer be considered as such and may develop into a social compromise. Although it is permissible to query whether the followers of the major religions have understood the true meaning of their sacred texts, this is very different from accusing them of falsifying them for their own ends.

In the battle for hearts and minds, a major challenge for most religious authorities came with the publication of Charles Darwin's book *On the Origin of Species* in 1859. The book immediately caused a stir in both the scientific community and the established Church, and the debate rolls on today. But instead of studying Darwin's Theory of Evolution with the understanding that it is indeed a theory and contains many queries yet to be resolved, many evolutionists resist alternative viewpoints and are thus in danger of themselves becoming entrenched. It is as if they are fearful of examining new ideas. Fortunately for them, there are several notable scientists and researchers who are not satisfied that Darwin's theory is foolproof. How good is the science that portrays Darwin's theory as complete, and that life as we know it can only have developed through fierce competition without any form of guidance or direction? Here then, is a grand opportunity to open our minds and to bring evolutionists and religionists together in harmony, although it may well be an uneasy alliance at first. Consider the following from the teachings of 'Abdu'l-Bahá:

> All beings, whether large or small, were created perfect and complete from the first, but their perfections appear in them by degrees. The organization of God is one: the evolution of existence is one: the divine system is one. Whether they be small or great beings, all are subject to one law and system. Each seed has in it from the first all the vegetable perfections. For example, in the seed all the vegetable perfections exist from the beginning, but not visibly; afterwards little by little they appear. So it is first the shoot which appears from the seed, then the branches, leaves, blossoms, and fruits; but from the beginning of its existence all these things are in the seed, potentially, though not apparently.

> In the same way, the embryo possesses from the first all perfections, such as the spirit, the mind, the sight, the smell, the taste – in one word, all the powers – but they are not visible, and become so only by degrees.

> Similarly, the terrestrial globe from the beginning was created with all its elements, substances, minerals, atoms, and organisms; but these only appeared by degrees: first the mineral, then the plant, afterward the animal, and finally man. But from the first these kinds and species existed, but

were undeveloped in the terrestrial globe, and then appeared only gradually. For the supreme organization of God, and the universal natural system, surrounds all beings, and all are subject to this rule. When you consider this universal system, you see that there is not one of the beings, which at its coming into existence has reached the limit of perfection. No, they gradually grow and develop, and then attain the degree of perfection.[17]

Atheists make the claim that religion is not so much revealed to us but invented by us. This can easily be disproved by reference to history, to the progressive nature of religious teachings that led in some cases to the formation of different religions and sects, and in many instances the fulfilment of prophecy. One challenge is to find what exactly atheists are trying to achieve; their present goals appear to be rather negative and whilst they are perfectly entitled to their viewpoint, religion is too powerful and lasting a force to be denied. Likewise, the teachings of philosophers are consistently challenged or modified and seldom last in their original form. The teachings revealed by the founders of the major religions go far beyond what our philosophers can or have produced in the way of guidance for humanity. The knowledge brought by the Manifestations of God has led to the gradual spiritual development of humanity. Unfortunately, history is also littered with man-made attempts at creating a religion, but these usually turn out to be a mish-mash of different religious doctrines and metaphysics and one cannot really discuss them without causing offence.

Knowledge has also had its dark side. Science and ethics are often uncomfortable bedfellows and their disagreements have contributed as much to war and suffering as politics has. In the pursuit of knowledge and discovery, science will defend research into more powerful ways of killing and will sometimes push the boundaries of probity in research – especially in experimentation on animals. The Nazi regime became involved in obscene experimentation on humans that even involved helpless children and prisoners.

Still, when we use the term 'science', we mean to include all the disciplines in the age-old search for knowledge. Most scientists have a viewpoint on how the world was created and challenge the creation theories. Some will feel that they have enough 'proof' to dispute the existence of God and others will have had their faith reinforced through their investigations and studies; there is probably no sure way to come to a conclusion that would suit everybody. Knowledge is a double-edged sword. The human mind grapples with all manner of problems; and because we have free will and the power to reason we have the opportunity to consider different viewpoints and express them, unless we have the misfortune to live under a tyrannical system that punishes those who deviate and this includes both extremist religious and political regimes. But as Ninian Smart points out, reason alone is sometimes not enough:

> Reason can demonstrate the existence of God but the masses need to have the truth given to them in symbolic form and this is the task of the Prophet . . . But there can ultimately be no question of a conflict between science and religion.[18]

2

Evolution and Civilization

Whether to believe in what religion teaches us is an age-old problem that was dealt with in the past by a good dose of fear and damnation. Atonement for sin could be used as a form of blackmail when the church had more power; and similar pressures are still brought to bear on believers by some of the more extreme clerics in some cultures. Perhaps because of this, atheists tend to ridicule the idea that sound religious teaching and greater spirituality would be a good basis for a healthy society; they firmly believe that humanity can manage ethics and moral principles without religion.

Whether we choose religion or science (in a society that allows choice and does not use the charge of apostasy as a means of oppression), we are free to accept or reject. Although Dawkins points out that some religious authorities will even target children to ensure that they can control hearts and minds, he ignores the fact that atheists are equally guilty in this respect. In such cases, the advantage surely lies with religion, insofar as the object is (or should be) to teach morals and good behaviour. Everywhere, even in so-called 'primitive' cultures, there are duties of parents towards their children, and theft and murder are prohibited. Surely the answer to building a just society lies in working to achieve harmony between religion and science and encouraging the opposing factions to consult in a non-conflictual way. Both value systems would obviously gain much from mutual understanding, greatly enriching society. In a lecture in 2003, Professor Suheil Bushrui stated that it cannot be denied that the nineteenth century saw many advances in science and technology, but it was also characterized by spiritual doubt and loss of faith in conventional religion, as is apparent from the writings of Friedrich Nietzsche and of Matthew Arnold, to name but two. Among those who noted the paradox of faith in a materialistic and rationalistic climate was Søren Kierkegaard, who stated, 'If I am capable of grasping God objectively, I do not believe, but precisely because I cannot do this I must believe.'

But this declaration of the limitations of reason and objectivity was the expression of a deeply critical and unfashionable outlook. The wilful separation of the intellect from spirituality reached its apotheosis under the pre-eminently evil socio-political systems of the twentieth century, Fascism and Communism. Those ideologies both proclaimed the infallibility of human attributes and numbered among their most ardent proponents men who were by training or aspiration intellectuals, including Lenin, Stalin, Goebbels and Mussolini. The Nazi death camps and the Communist gulags are terrible monuments to an intellect untempered by morality, and an intellectual impulse which values people only to the extent that they serve The Idea, whatever political form it may take. Notwithstanding the great contributions that the rational faculty can make to the progress and development of man, its power bereft of the divine spark of humanity is brutally dangerous and destructive.[1]

The loss of values is also evident in the proliferation of pornographic literature, third-rate music, anti-social behaviour and some modern films. Trying to stem the tide of anti-social behaviour and violent crime with political (vote-seeking) ideas seems to be an ineluctable part of modern democracy. We should instead be reaffirming that there is a spiritual side to our nature that can be nurtured with the right approach and teachings that would invoke sympathy, empathy and compassion. Even the 'scientific' approach (psychology) has some merit because it can sometimes force us to think about spiritual alternatives that have often been set aside in the race for material knowledge and possessions. 'Love thy neighbour' (or at least consider your neighbour's point of view), the Golden Rule, has been present in all the religions.

Must we really accept that because the basic principle of evolution has shown us that the world of being is very ancient and was not created just a few thousand years ago, it negates the raison d'être of religious teachings and moral guidance? What then is the justification for our existence? We should be teaching both sides of this debate in greater detail and reevaluating the message.

Atheism became reputable under Communism, a system that stifled religion in many ways. Indeed, Communists were angry and wary of the power that religion often had over the minds of the citizens that they themselves wanted to control. Yet Communism had a certain religious fervour of its own and a vested interest in the techniques of brainwashing to rid itself of opposition.

Although politically, both at the national and international level, racial tensions can be a major consequence of fanaticism, the broader issues of trade and finance are often able to rise above that narrow vision. Race hatred and abuse can sometimes drive a wedge between the followers of religions, but it is as well to remember that one of the most horrific examples of racial hatred was given free rein under an atheistic regime – Nazism., which also had a pseudo-religious overtone. The regime attempted to use a 'scientific' approach to racial purity (sometimes adopting eugenics) and developed a form of ethics that demanded obedience to a hierarchy that was seeking the elusive perfect political system for control of the population.

Fascism, Nazism, Communism, and indeed many other 'isms', although able to impose discipline by draconian means, have been shown to be morally corrupt and spiritually impoverished; in effect, sterile man-made systems of ethics. The state therefore has a duty to create the right conditions for true religion to survive and thrive as a bulwark against totalitarianism, crime and iniquity.

Purpose and process

Atheism relies heavily on science and evolutionary theory to bolster its claims and although we cannot argue with the central theme of evolution, it does not prove that there is no God or Creator. Nor can a religious person or theist prove to the satisfaction of everybody that God or a Creator is the Prime Mover, but the belief that there is a purpose to life gives the advantage to the theist.

When we go back to the earliest records of religious teachings and attempt a study of their core message together with the social development of the human race, we are able to see it as a *process*. Knowledge and ideas about how we should live our lives and interact with each other have been, and will always be, of a progressive nature; we move by degrees to a higher level of interaction and social bonding. Some will disagree with this observation, and some will always resist change, but many historians point to evidence that there was and is a purpose behind the development of human society. Religion has certainly been a major factor in this. Development and social progress has been recognized as being progressive, and their relationship as vital to humanity, emphasizing that there is a purpose to life that is not always evident in atheistic arguments.

Apart from this, a major question that has bothered philosophers for generations is: What is the purpose of life? Can religion provide the answer? Or science? Or will it be atheists? One writer who alludes to this question which 'continues to lurk in the background' is Hoff Conow:

The various branches of science continue to restrict themselves to this same obsolete either/or universe by their reluctance to attribute original causation to an unknown Intelligence. Nonetheless, they remain vitally concerned with the **effects** this non-existent cause has produced. Somehow, purpose continues to lurk in the background along with **meaning** to haunt them. Any causal explanation of any phenomenon (effect) immediately opens the door to its meaning. It is not difficult to take the next step and surmise that what has meaning very likely has purpose, to issues that some scientists try to avoid by substituting 'function' for purpose, and relegating 'meaning' to information or data. Others have realized that the quest for information is not the same as the quest for knowledge and wisdom.[2]

One interesting thing about the theory of evolution is that it has shown that there has been a direction; a relentless move towards improvement in all forms of life that would assist progress and development. This process finally led to the appearance of the human species that could utilize and develop the resources of the earth. With the right teachings and guidance, the process will bring into existence a true world civilization, according to the Bahá'í teachings.

Pierre Teilhard de Chardin tried to integrate the current theories of evolution with Christian theology. Of Chardin's views Fritjof Capra writes:

His key concept is what he called the 'Law of Complexity-Consciousness,' which states that evolution proceeds in the direction of increasing complexity, and that this increase in complexity is accompanied by a corresponding rise of consciousness, culminating in human spirituality. Teilhard used the term 'consciousness' in the sense of awareness and defines it as 'the specific effect of organized complexity,' which is perfectly compatible with the systems view of mind.[3]

Finally, he saw God as the source of all being, and in particular as the source of the evolutionary force. In view of the systems concept of God as the universal dynamics of self-organisation, we can say that among the many images mystics have used to describe the Divine, Teilhard's concept of God, if liberated from its patriarchal connotations, may well be the one that comes closest to the views of modern science.[4]

Using evolutionary theory, one could postulate that the development of mind and intelligence was vital to fully utilize the concepts and teachings that are necessary for the advance of civilization, and that it appeared naturally. It also brought with it free will, something that other species lack, as they are trapped by their instincts and desires. Paradoxically, this has allowed humanity to express free will in a negative way, by interpreting the religious teachings according to its own interests and even rejecting religion altogether, denying God! There can be no greater test than this for humanity. And, as described by Esslemont, it is an unnecessary conflict:

> Bahá'u'lláh confirms the scientists who claim, not six thousand, but millions and billions of years for the history of the earth's creation. The evolution theory does not deny creative power. It only tries to describe the method of its manifestation; and the wonderful story of the material universe which the astronomer, the geologist, the physicist and the biologist are gradually unfolding to our gaze is, rightly appreciated, far more capable of evoking the deepest reverence and worship than the crude and bald account of creation given in the Hebrew Scriptures. The old account in the Book of Genesis had, however, the advantage of indicating by a few bold strokes of symbolism the essential spiritual meanings of the story, as a master painter may, by a few strokes of the brush, convey expressions which the mere plodder with the most

laborious attention to details may utterly fail to portray. If the material details blind us to the spiritual meaning then we should be better without them, but if we have once firmly grasped the essential meaning of the whole scheme, then knowledge of the details will give our conception a wonderful added richness and splendour and make it a magnificent picture instead of a mere sketch plan.[5]

As for the much-debated theory of intelligent design, 'Abdu'l-Bahá explained that no matter what form or shape our evolutionary ancestors had:

> the animal having preceded man is not a proof of the evolution, change and alteration of the species, nor that man was raised from the animal world to the human world. For while the individual appearance of these different beings is certain, it is possible that man came into existence after the animal. So when we examine the vegetable kingdom, we see that the fruits of the different trees do not arrive at maturity at one time; on the contrary, some come first and others afterwards. This priority does not prove that the later fruit of one tree was produced from the earlier fruit of another tree.[6]

We shall return to this explanation later.

Moral evolution

It is common practice to think that a religious person is a spiritual person and that spirituality is an aspect of their faith, yet a person may well be concerned about spiritual matters without being affiliated to a religion. Conversely, a religious person can be so fanatical and overzealous about rules and traditions that the spiritual part of his faith eludes him. It is a subject that can cause much debate, especially in this age when terrorist activity takes place in the name of religion. Yet what proof supports the opposing claims of exclusivity by one religion over another? Why are most opposed to change? Why should they clash? It is a fact that without commitment and unified action success in any endeavour is limited.

We appear to have had the ability to bond emotionally and socially very early on in our evolution and even as early as hunter-gatherer societies, although some may dispute this. Without a doubt, religion has helped groups of people to bond, but the way some groups or ideologies achieve this may sometimes be by force or intimidation. This inevitably leads to resistance and antagonism, and given an opportunity some will create alternative sects. To be exiled or made an outcast was often the ultimate weapon against anti-social behaviour. It was a prospect that could only be countered by the exiles gathering sufficient support to fight back or developing superior ideas and philosophies that enabled them to form (successful) rival groups. When a section of the community falls prey to ruthless and/or fanatical leadership, and particularly when new ideas are introduced, there is the possibility of violent reaction and a split will generally occur. New ideas or philosophies can also be a reaction to a new teaching from a religious innovator.

People constantly blame religion as having been a major cause of war and dissension, but when we speak of religious wars it surely it is more truthful to say that wars have been waged in which religion was used as the excuse – when for example, different shades of interpretation have been magnified to arouse the baser instincts and gain support for the creation of another leader and thus, another sect. This is ammunition for critics of religion.

Religious and indeed political leaders have always had the power to intimidate and utilize subtle means of persuasion to accomplish their objectives, and are often disingenuous enough to use religion for this end. Authoritative leaders, for the sake of power and fame, consistently usurp the role of religion, using the hold that religion has on the minds of the people and misinterpreting its writings for a political agenda. Such manipulation has sometimes caused religious groups to fragment and form sects. This in itself surely shows that it is often a distortion of religious teachings that can be responsible for causing disunity and even war. Moreover, some of the interpretations they give may border on the incredible, and are often made by self-deluded experts deftly manipulating the texts and producing results that are accepted by simple-minded and extremely gullible people who find it difficult to question. These may fall victim to charges of apostasy if they try to oppose, so that they become fearful of punishment both in this world and in the hereafter. This too brings ridicule on religion from atheists or philosophers, although science too has experienced similar deviations; caused by malpractice and oppression.

Human progress has always been enriched by religion, as 'Abdu'l-Bahá explains:

Although a man may progress in science and philosophy, if he does not take advantage of the power of the spirit, he is incomplete.

Moses was neither a philosopher nor a scientist. Outwardly he was but a simple shepherd, but he was able to instruct and develop a whole nation which had been in a state of demoralization; but which through his influence reached a very enlightened civilization. Jesus Christ did not come from the world of princes or scientists. Outwardly he was but an humble artisan, his disciples simple fishermen. Why were these disciples able to do what philosophers and scientists failed to accomplish? You have the example in Peter who was assisted by the Holy Spirit, as have been all those who have enlightened humanity – for universal education can be accomplished only through the Holy Spirit.

Mohammed through his power was enabled to elevate a

nation, for on his teachings a mighty civilization was constructed in the Arabian peninsula, the influence of which, as recorded in history, extended as far west as Spain. Let us be just. When a being, alone, in the midst of a savage tribe begins by teaching them and finally succeeds in raising them to a high degree of civilization, we must admit that he has an extraordinary power. What I mean is this – philosophy and science will not suffice to elevate and civilize a people who are in a bestial condition.

What philosophy has ever elevated a whole nation and influenced humanity? Philosophy of necessity is restricted to a small school and cannot have an essentially moral influence.[7]

Udo Schaefer in *Bahá'í Ethics in the Light of Scripture* reminds us that the Revelation of Bahá'u'lláh also has a political dimension in that it provides guidance for a new world order. Progress in the political realm, where the equilibrium of society is upset by the arrival of new teachings, is generally slow and although there was a surge in the heyday of Islamic culture, the eighteenth and nineteenth centuries saw not only a general upheaval amongst the rulers of the world, but the biggest leap in inventions and discoveries in the whole history of the human race. Maybe some will say that progress has mainly been material, but this is a by-product of the spiritual teachings once a new message has freed society from certain hindrances and prompted a new way of looking at the world. The problems of the past have arisen when the teachings have been misunderstood, or taken over by a dominant, power-seeking hierarchy of priests. Scientists are encouraged to re-examine data when it does not provide the right answer. Religious teachers should do the same. In the words of 'Abdu'l-Bahá,

Praise be to God! The mediaeval ages of darkness have passed away and this century of radiance has dawned, this century wherein the reality of things is becoming evident, wherein science is penetrating the mysteries of the universe, the oneness of the world of humanity is being established, and service to mankind is the paramount motive of all existence.[8]

In 2008 the winner of the Templeton Prize for Progress toward Research or discoveries about Spirituality Realities was Michael Heller, a Polish cosmologist and Catholic priest. He was quoted as saying, 'Science gives us knowledge of the world and religion gives us meaning.' He also said,

> The standard theory of evolution ascribes a lot of results to chance, whereas adherents of intelligent design say instead that everything should be planned by God. What is a random event? It is something which is of low probability that nevertheless happens. I don't see any conflict between chance events and God's planning of the universe.[9]

Is there anything in Darwin's theory or modern studies that say species can be shown to have evolved into other species? 'Abdu'l-Bahá's explanation is as follows:

> Certain European philosophers agree that the species grows and develops, and that even change and alteration are also possible. One of the proofs that they give for this theory is that through the attentive study and verification of the science of geology it has become clear that the existence of the vegetable preceded that of the animal, and that of the animal preceded that of man. They admit that both the vegetable and the animal species have changed, for in some of the strata of the earth they have discovered plants which existed in the past and are now extinct; they have progressed, grown in strength, their form and appearance have changed, and so the species have altered. In the same way, in the strata of the earth there are some species of animals which have

changed and are transformed . . . The principal argument is this: that the existence of traces of members proves that they once existed, and as now they are no longer of service, they have gradually disappeared. Therefore, while the perfect and necessary members have remained, those which are unnecessary have gradually disappeared by the modification of the species, but the traces of them continue.

The first answer to this argument is the fact that the animal having preceded man is not a proof of the evolution, change and alteration of the species, nor that man was raised from the animal world to the human world. For while the individual appearance of these different beings is certain, it is possible that man came into existence after the animal. So when we examine the vegetable kingdom, we see that the fruits of the different trees do not arrive at maturity at one time; on the contrary, some come first and others afterward. This priority does not prove that the later fruit of one tree was produced from the earlier fruit of another tree.

Second, these slight signs and traces of members have perhaps a great reason of which the mind is not yet cognizant. How many things exist of which we do not yet know the reason! So the science of physiology – that is to say, the knowledge of the composition of the members – records that the reason and cause of the difference in the colours of animals, and of the hair of men, of the redness of the lips, and of the variety of the colours of birds, is still unknown; it is secret and hidden. But it is known that the pupil of the eye is black so as to attract the rays of the sun, for if it were another colour – that is, uniformly white – it would not attract the rays of the sun. Therefore, as the reason of the things we have mentioned is unknown, it is possible that the reason and the wisdom of these traces of members, whether they be in the animal or man, are equally unknown. Certainly there is a reason, even though it is not known.

Third, let us suppose that there was a time when some

animals, or even man, possessed some members which have now disappeared; this is not a sufficient proof of the change and evolution of the species. For man, from the beginning of the embryonic period till he reaches the degree of maturity, goes through different forms and appearances. His aspect, his form, his appearance and colour change; he passes from one form to another, and from one appearance to another. Nevertheless, from the beginning of the embryonic period he is of the species of man – that is to say, an embryo of a man and not of an animal; but this is not at first apparent, but later it becomes visible and evident. For example, let us suppose that man once resembled the animal, and that now he has progressed and changed. Supposing this to be true, it is still not a proof of the change of species. No, as before mentioned, it is merely like the change and alteration of the embryo of man until it reaches the degree of reason and perfection. We will state it more clearly. Let us suppose that there was a time when man walked on his hands and feet, or had a tail; this change and alteration is like that of the fetus in the womb of the mother. Although it changes in all ways, and grows and develops until it reaches the perfect form, from the beginning it is a special species. We also see in the vegetable kingdom that the original species of the genus do not change and alter, but the form, colour and bulk will change and alter, or even progress.

To recapitulate: as man in the womb of the mother passes from form to form, from shape to shape, changes and develops, and is still the human species from the beginning of the embryonic period – in the same way man, from the beginning of his existence in the matrix of the world, is also a distinct species – that is, man – and has gradually evolved from one form to another. Therefore, this change of appearance, this evolution of members, this development and growth, even though we admit the reality of growth and progress, does not prevent the species from being original.

Man from the beginning was in this perfect form and composition, and possessed capacity and aptitude for acquiring
material and spiritual perfections, and was the manifestation
of these words, 'We will make man in Our image and likeness.'[10]

Knowledge and purpose

Can knowledge really be defined just by equating it with learning and reasoning? There is surely an innate desire to learn
that helped us to advance from the primitive conditions of
early history and evolved exponentially as humanity evolved.
This is evolution at work that is a little different from the
physical challenges that Darwin observed. It is an evolution
that highlights an ability to learn in human terms, involving
imagination and a yearning for knowledge that vastly exceeds
other life forms. Human knowledge also has the advantage of
expression; this is seen in our poetry and music and can often
be equated with 'spirituality'. There is also conscience, humility, emotion and philosophical thought. These higher feelings,
when exposed to the right teachings, can be extremely powerful. This is the real you that can be realized in meditation and
contemplation.

Altruism surely cannot be fully explained by genes? If so,
was it prompted by continuous communal activity or social
bonding that prompted a mutation, or was it inherited from
some ancient source as part of the natural evolutionary necessity that was to lead inexorably to humanity as we know it
today? What then of the 'Selfish Gene'? Should it not be rede-
fined as the successful gene? Dawkins' book *The Selfish Gene*
was highly acclaimed, and his choice of title was also very
clever, playing off (in a form of propaganda really) the fact
that the genes have to be 'selfish' to survive. Unfortunately,
some have expanded the metaphor to state that 'we' are born
selfish.

The introduction of moral behaviour into society via religious teachings therefore appears to clash with the selfish gene prognosis. However, Dawkins explained in a footnote that it was a misunderstanding of what he was trying to say. Nevertheless, there is a tendency amongst many scientists who are committed to atheism to distort the findings that come with their research so that they appear to confirm that there is no need for belief in God, and Dawkins is not averse to this approach.

Evolution is a wonderful theory, but should be considered as the beginning of research and not the final episode in trying to understand our origins and destiny. Isn't that what religious teachings are all about? Many have made the spiritual journey, undergone a transformation and made the transition from despair to hope. For some it is easy, for others it is hard. To paraphrase John Donne, no man (or woman) is an island; we need each other in many ways and for many things. Sometimes we need to identify ourselves and others by race, politics, family, tribe or religion. Of these, the most powerful has been family, closely followed by religion even though true spirituality at the core of the religion is not easy to define. But ordinary people *inherit* their religion. It is a badge of honour that they will in certain situations defend to their death, and in other cases will abandon, as many have today.

Both atheists and theists have concepts that they cling to tenaciously. One cannot doubt the sincerity or intelligence of atheists generally. But humanity discriminates – God does not. The common denominator for humanity is that all may contribute to the material advancement of humanity whether they believe in God or not. The fact that we have free will (God-given) allows us all to accept or reject.

When religious beliefs are condemned it is usually because some of the older teachings seem outdated and do not quite fit in with changing conditions, and the critics are concerned more about these outward 'trappings'. They may be right to be concerned about some of the social teachings and laws, but the spiritual teachings are for all time. Still, these teachings are often wrapped in metaphor or analogy, and when this fact is not understood these too can become a stumbling block.

Since God is beyond human comprehension, the Manifestations of God have had to use terminology that was acceptable for the age they lived in, putting their message into words that may appear simple in some instances until you consider the many meanings or levels of meaning.

Literal interpretations of scripture were perhaps acceptable in the past; they were surely meant to be illustrations that would appeal to devoted followers. Helping the (*spiritually*) blind to understand teachings and thus be enlightened, or the (*spiritually*) dead to become alive to the message or teachings are two examples. All religions are beset by doubts and questions from their followers and stories or fables have always been used to illustrate difficult precepts, followed by guidelines that would help the 'blind to see' and the 'dead' to be quickened. However, such examples, when they are promoted as literal fact, are eagerly seized upon by atheists as evidence of superstition. We will need to be more specific in defending religion.

With regard to the New Testament, no original exists, although there are many copies of the alleged original material. It is impossible to discover how many interpretations might have crept in over the centuries that could have changed the original meaning, and unfortunately atheists, in seeking to dismiss religious history as fantasy, use this. Some translations of the Old Testament, mainly Hebrew with some Aramaic, may have been made around the 3rd century BC, but there has naturally been much dispute and research over the centuries. Creationism is not by any means a biblical *doctrine* but an interpretation by some Christians and Jews of a creation story that suited the mind-set of people of long ago. Likewise, the resurrection of Jesus has been subjected to various explanations. Old Testament stories that highlight the great age of the prophets (sometimes in hundreds of years) surely relate to the time-span of the message that they brought to their people, before a later prophet renewed it, and not to their physical age. What was always necessary was a reliable conduit that could convey instructions or guidelines to the believers. That conduit would be a Prophet or Messenger and their words would be in a style that could be comprehended at that time.

The spiritual verities that have constantly been renewed in the various revelations have been eventually absorbed into everyday life and society. Should we mock a child who believes childish things? We must remember that the child is taught by adults, who are themselves struggling to explain something in a childish language. It takes a certain expertise to do this.

But we are now living in an age when the literal interpretation of religious scripture is no longer acceptable.

> When I was a child, I spake as a child, I understood as a child, I thought as a child: but when I became a man, I put away childish things.[11]

Psychologists realize that religion serves certain needs that do not always change with the growth of knowledge. Faith can provide certainty and stability at crucial moments, and a misunderstanding of this need is a common failing of science and atheism. The physical evolution of the human race is as nothing compared to the spiritual, and there will always be the eternal quest for the meaning of life. It has also been well documented that people can change themselves with a religious input into their lives; this is not so easy with just a scientific/psychological approach.

Perhaps it is as well that atheists do not believe in an afterlife, as they have no way of explaining or understanding, as a theist would, that life is a journey, with a destination. They cannot agree on the necessity for the journey *or* the destination. If we cannot understand life, or the meaning of life, how can we understand or accept that death is not final, but a continuation? Near-death experiences are eagerly examined by those who would like answers. Nevertheless, it is the inspiration that believers seek from their religious belief that sustains them, as Bahá'u'lláh describes:

> There can be no doubt whatever that the peoples of the world, of whatever race or religion, derive their inspiration from one heavenly Source, and are the subjects of one God. The difference between the ordinances under which they abide should be attributed to the varying requirements and exigencies of the age in which they were revealed. All of them, except a few which are the outcome of human perversity, were ordained of God, and are a reflection of His Will and Purpose.[12]

The mystics of every religion have always been aware that the Creator is unknowable insofar as the human mind is unable to grasp such concepts. Bahá'u'lláh confirms this:

> To every discerning and illuminated heart it is evident that God, the unknowable Essence, the Divine Being, is immensely exalted beyond every human attribute, such as corporeal existence, ascent and descent, egress and regress. Far be it from His glory that human tongue should adequately recount His praise, or that human heart comprehend His fathomless mystery. He is, and hath ever been, veiled in the ancient eternity of His Essence, and will remain in His Reality everlastingly hidden from the sight of men. 'No vision taketh in Him, but He taketh in all vision; He is the Subtle, the All-Perceiving.'[13]

No wonder it has always been impossible to 'explain' God! For example, the Old Testament did not name God and it was considered sacrilege to try.

Civilizations gradually disintegrate when their belief systems are so watered down that they become meaningless; we have many examples in our modern society. Darwin referred to the survival of the fittest, and although it can be shown from his work that this allowed some groups in the animal kingdom to triumph over others it also shows that much may be gained by cooperating. If it is analysed in this way, and can be offered as an example of the advantages gained by overcoming some of the challenges of diversity, it shows merit of a different sort. We can say that Darwin revolutionized our understanding of evolution and our origins, but at the same time many of his supporters assumed that this was a mighty blow to the faith of millions. Atheists were quick to take up the theory and throw it in the faces of those who believed in God. They were far too hasty. More is achieved by unity and cooperation.

3

The Search for Truth

Know thou that, according to what thy Lord, the Lord of all men, hath decreed in His Book, the favours vouchsafed by Him unto mankind have been, and will ever remain, limitless in their range. First and foremost among these favours, which the Almighty hath conferred upon man, is the gift of understanding. His purpose in conferring such a gift is none other except to enable His creature to know and recognize the one true God – exalted be His glory. This gift giveth man the power to discern the truth in all things, leadeth him to that which is right, and helpeth him to discover the secrets of creation.[1]

Bahá'u'lláh

How does a simple person with no scientific qualifications convince committed atheists that creation had a divine Mover? On reflection, he or she probably doesn't need to – it is atheists who are desperate for explanations that will convince others that they are right. They seem to lack that inner conviction that brings peace to a believer. Are atheists searching or just rejecting?

In discussing God, perhaps a more acceptable term today is 'ultimate reality'. Though unknowable, this Reality is the driving force behind everything that can be observed in nature and in the vastness of the universe that is now being opened to our gaze by increasingly powerful telescopes and technology. And it is through the Messengers or Manifestations of God that we may have a glimpse of God's attributes and influence on the world of humanity. Why can't atheists accept this possibility and adjust a more conciliatory tone?

It is natural for scientists to seek proof; that is the nature of their profession. But how is it possible to find proof of a Creator? Everything that we can visualize comes from human experience or imagination, but that is not God. However, the task of the scientist in unravelling the secrets of nature for the benefit of humankind is informed by the creative spirit, as 'Abdu'l-Bahá affirms:

> Electricity was once a latent force of nature. According to nature's laws it should remain a hidden secret, but the spirit of man discovered it, brought it forth from its secret depository and made its phenomena visible. It is evident and manifest that man is capable of breaking nature's laws. How does he accomplish it? Through a spirit with which God has endowed him at creation. This is a proof that the spirit of man differentiates and distinguishes him above all the lower kingdoms. It is this spirit to which the verse in the Old Testament refers when it states, 'And God said, Let us make man in our image, after our likeness.' The spirit of man alone penetrates the realities of God and partakes of the divine bounties.[2]

The search for knowledge is to be human, and asking questions also helps to develop faith. Unfortunately, those who seek a spiritual solution to their questions are often confused by a plethora of religious movements offering answers that are usually linked to the promise of a better life and future only if you follow their way of life. Of course, this rather gloomy criticism can also be applied to commercial and political promises of the vision that our modern material world offers, with the constant emphasis on possessions and wealth. It is a shallow vision. There has to be something greater, some hope of a solution, a target to aim for.

Religion has always provided a community with a common support and attempts to inject meaning into their lives. While there have been many errors, these have usually been caused by human weakness or misunderstanding – and we have seen similar errors in scientific and political fields that have been the cause of much suffering. There has to be a solution that offers justice to all.

Of course, there are many who do not believe in God and still have strong ethical views, but what is the origin of those views? The impetus has come from religious teachings! When searching for truth a great many philosophers fall into the trap called pride. Although we can see the logic of value systems made by reasoning for the good of society, the problem is finding the boundaries that are acceptable to society and how they fit with the political will of those in power. Millions of vulnerable people, seeking love, care, trust and security, have been deprived through the various political (and even religious) systems that have come to power in various parts of the world. Communist and Fascist regimes both failed miserably in that arena; they created their own (sometimes barbaric) systems of jurisprudence and control that were extremely sinister and alienated many from the basic values that they would have preferred. 'Abdu'l-Bahá explains why:

> The prophets are sent to refresh the dead body of the world, to render the dumb eloquent, to give peace to the troubled, to make illumined the indifferent and to set free from the material world all beings who are its captives. Leave a child to himself and he becomes ill-mannered and thoughtless. He must be shown the path, so that he may become acquainted with the world of the soul – the world of divine gifts.[3]

Many anti-social people seem to have no firm religious belief or only the slightest understanding of the meaning and purpose of religion, and are the first to react against laws or moral principles that are imposed on them. But a society without acceptable and enforceable morals becomes a broken society. There has to be general acceptance that the government or those in authority have the right to impose such laws and to see that justice prevails. The '*disaffected youth*' syndrome, for which those in government and the different professions can only really offer counselling or medication, creates large numbers of young people with little or no concern for social values and respect for authority, and certainly very little interest in religion.

There are, however, heroic instances of individuals who make sacrifices to help young people extricate themselves from such backgrounds and manage to achieve success, when governments cannot. One such example is Camilla Batmanghelidjh who founded Kids Company in London and has had extraordinary success in tackling problems at the source. Many other grass-roots projects have achieved what political institutions cannot. Those who run them seem to have an inner strength and commitment that sets them aside from others. It is interesting that such people have found a way to communicate with and change the attitudes of disaffected young people, whilst government bodies, including social services with all the 'expertise' and funds at their disposal, often fail miserably. It is a commitment that develops from supreme confidence, ability and a spiritual certitude.

A musical project that started in Venezuela in 1975, called *El Systema*, has had phenomenal success in reaching out to children from poverty-stricken areas, saving many thousands from a life of crime and delinquency. A large question that should be asked is: can drug abuse possibly be targeted more successfully by religious teachings? This has been tried in some areas, for instance in Swindon in the United Kingdom through the Tranquillity Zones and the Young People's Empowerment Programme, and shown to have had some success. More research and support from government is definitely needed. Thoughtful people are realizing that it is not morality which leads to religion, but religion to morality, and that the structure of morality collapses when its foundation, religion, is destroyed.

Unfortunately modern society is veering toward a sterile existence based upon man-made rules, and there is a growing ignorance of the virtues that are meant to sustain humankind in a peaceful coexistence. The overwhelming impact of technological innovation has left a large section of humanity floundering in moral confusion over the latest 'must have' gadgets, apps and computer games. Much time and money has also been invested in treating the effects of alcohol and drug abuse.. Not so much is invested in cultivating a search for moral alternatives.

> The vitality of men's belief in God is dying out in every land; nothing short of His wholesome medicine can ever restore it. The corrosion of ungodliness is eating into the vitals of human society; what else but the Elixir of His potent Revelation can cleanse and revive it? Is it within human power, O Ḥakím, to effect in the constituent elements of any of the minute and indivisible particles of matter so complete a transformation as to transmute it into purest gold? Perplexing and difficult as this may appear, the still greater task of converting satanic strength into heavenly power is one that We have been empowered to accomplish. The Force capable of such a transformation transcendeth the potency of the Elixir itself. The Word of God, alone, can claim the distinction of being endowed with the capacity required for so great and far-reaching a change.[4]

But this origin of morality in human society has been questioned by Dawkins, and he is just one of many who would like to show that there is a Darwinian solution that could reinforce atheist claims.

Of course there have always been problems with anti-social

behaviour, most of which stems from poverty and ignorance; it is not just a modern phenomena. Apart from the moral deprivation that afflicts those who are on the periphery of society, there are also those who have access to wealth but for one reason or another opt out of normal community life and grow up oblivious to the values that could guide them. Their attitude to drugs and alcohol are bad examples for youth. There used to be some control from the guidance of religious authority, when the church held sway over the lives of the people, and although in some areas of the world this is still partly true, the rising power of extremist movements that give power to pseudo-religious teachings is having disastrous effects. The insidious influence of terrorist groups who justify their violent struggle for power by claiming that it is a religious duty is undermining progress in many societies. When such extreme attitudes are justified by religion it is no surprise that atheists use this to attack belief in God.

Nevertheless, aside from the extremism that is now affecting all the older religions, there are beginning to appear signs and opportunities for sharing common values that are at the heart of all religious systems. Since the 19th century there has been an upheaval in all the major religions and the effects are still with us, accompanied by uncertainty as to what it will lead to. Quite recently, many revivalist movements have sprung up that are trying to reach out to those who feel their lives have been blighted; thus helping them to reintegrate with society. So how do they propose to treat people who have turned against society and have a complete disregard for moral values? Is it a problem that can be solved by religion? Can it be left to the politicians?

Training

A young person without training may be likened to an uncut stone that to the untrained eye is an unattractive rock. To a physicist the stone contains myriads of molecules that are seemingly random and not immediately useful. For a builder, there is the potential for a number of projects. For a sculptor, there are endless possibilities to fashion stone into an object of beauty. A religious person may see the possibility that this young person, or 'rock', that they believe has a soul, could be trained, using the teachings revealed by the ultimate Fashioner, to ultimately become a pillar of society. 'Abdu'l-Bahá describes this process:

> Know thou that every soul is fashioned after the nature of God, each being pure and holy at his birth. Afterwards, however, the individuals will vary according to what they acquire of virtues or vices in this world. Although all existent beings are in their very nature created in ranks or degrees, for capacities are various, nevertheless every individual is born holy and pure, and only thereafter may he become defiled.[5]

And in the writings of Bahá'u'lláh we find this significant statement:

> Through the mere revelation of the word 'Fashioner', issuing forth from His lips and proclaiming His attribute to mankind, such power is released as can generate, through successive ages, all the manifold arts which the hands of man can produce.[6]

Morality has slipped anchor, the consciences of young people have been cast adrift and the need for a sensitive religious input has never been greater. The overwhelmingly sterile existence of modern life, based upon man-made rules, is sowing confusion in the minds of many and can easily lead to a turbulent or abusive family background, mental health issues, school exclusion, or drug and alcohol dependency. But given the right teaching and opportunities our young people can change the world. The 'purpose of religion', said 'Abdu'l-Bahá, 'is the acquisition of praiseworthy virtues, the betterment of morals, the spiritual development of mankind, the real life and divine bestowals.'[7] 'The purpose of divine revelation is the education of humanity,'[8] as writer Udo Schaefer succinctly puts it in *The Clash of Religions.*

In the 19th century few would have realized that their seemingly stable world system was soon to be swept away. Thrones toppled across Europe as dynasties fell and borders changed. Many will have wondered what would replace them. It certainly did not lead to an end to war, or the possibility of greater unity. The religious communities were themselves bewildered – without making major changes to their belief systems, the major religions of the old world order could not work together or embrace any meaningful system that could lead to peace and world unity. For too long they had been steeped in superstition and distorted messages. This has led to widespread unbelief, and the New Atheists naturally utilize it to bolster their own claims.

We should let the fetters of religion be loosened and the mental shutters be opened so that the light of true faith may enter our homes and our lives to bring unity. We can now travel to the far reaches of the earth, yet we are separate – community life has deteriorated and neither atheism, nor nihilism, nor revolutionary political ideologies can possibly replace it with their hollow alternatives. Atheism always seems to lead to a dead end, with no substantial ideas for a better life, even though many famous people have paid lip service to its unresponsive belief system.

The poet Percy Bysshe Shelley was deliberately obtuse about his 'atheism' and merely observed that design should be proved before a designer can be inferred. He was not aware in his time of the immensity of the cosmos that is now being revealed with modern telescopes. Would he have had more insight if he had been able to accept that the immeasurable, unfathomable universe is a substantive proof of a grand design?

Throughout the universe the divine power is effulgent in endless images and pictures. The world of creation, the world of humanity may be likened to the earth itself and the divine power to the sun. This Sun has shone upon all mankind. In the endless variety of its reflections the divine Will is manifested.[9]

Moreover, the writings associated with the Prophets are revelations or communications from a supernatural source that were revealed to assist humanity in a way that would benefit them throughout eternity. If you cannot accept that revelation has a purpose and is progressive, with changes in social laws being an inevitable part of evolutionary change for social living and not based upon blind acceptance of tradition, then the truth will always be obscured. Social laws were introduced for a reason and for a particular age and situation.

When Dawkins speaks of change or *Zeitgeist* (the spirit of the time) he categorically denies that it has anything to do with religion, going right against the opinions and findings of eminent historians and philosophers. But he doesn't have an alternative:

We need to explain why the changing moral Zeitgeist is so widely synchronised across large numbers of people; and we need to explain its relatively consistent direction.[10]

I would ask that as a starting point he examines the concept of progressive revelation as outlined in the Bahá'í Faith and carry out a serious study of the *teachings* of the founders of the major religions (insofar as the original teachings can be studied) with the scientific rigour and analysis that he claims to believe in, rather than a juvenile attack on the chronicles.

Although there has been a lot of human interpretation that has skewed the original teachings of all the older religions, a spiritual interpretation of these allow for a more common-sense discernment of what is meant. Without this, if we accept the stories of old in a literal sense, we drift into the realm of conjecture, misunderstanding and even fantasy. Take for instance Dawkins' insistent misconception of stories of Noah's Ark, the parting of the Red Sea and the Creation scenarios.

Many of the traditions of modern times go right against the core teachings of religion, such as the marriage of cousins, honour killings, the status of women, and the general observance of customs that have no religious authenticity. These are examples of religion gone astray and not a sign that the original teachings are wrong. As Bahá'í writer Ulrich Gollmer explains:

> No religion comes into being in an historical and intellectual no-mans-land. Every religion addresses the needs of particular people. These people, however, are under the influence of traditional ways of thinking. Yet religious communication requires understanding. Hence, if a new religious content is to be conveyed, this can be done at first only through the use of existing models and customary thought patterns. Every new religion arises within the sphere of influence of an existing religious tradition, adopting or rejecting the images, terms, attitudes, motives and institutions of that tradition, sometimes developing them further, sometimes adding marginal or new elements, and thus developing its own specific tradition and its own religious language. In this sense religion – every religion – is syncretistic.[11]

Man is very ancient, the result of millions of years of evolution and, according to scriptures, created with a spiritual soul. In the hunter-gatherer stage the organization of food supplies could not sustain large groups, so fresh ideas and guidance were necessary to stimulate further progress. Teachings were revealed to lead humanity into agriculture and nomadism that allowed control of food supplies and the innovations that led to surplus products and trade – the birth of economics.

Atheists will dismiss the suggestion that all of this can be connected to religious teachings, but they are not able to disprove it. Some human attributes that cannot be isolated by scientists also give to us the realization and consciousness of self that animals do not possess, and this helps us to respond to the sensory experiences of music, poetry and art. In the words of the poet Khalil Gibran:

And a man said, Speak to us of self-knowledge.

And he answered, saying:
Your hearts know in silence the secrets of the days and the nights.
But your ears thirst for the sound of your heart's knowledge.
You would know in words that which you have always known in thought.
You would touch with your fingers the naked body of your dreams.

And it is well that you should.
The hidden well-spring of your soul must needs rise and run murmuring to the sea;
And the treasure of your infinite depths would be revealed to your eyes.
But let there be no scales to weigh your unknown treasure;
And seek not the depths of your knowledge with staff or sounding line.
For self is a sea boundless and measureless.[12]

At each stage in our evolution ethics and morals were essential to ensure a stable community. Where were they to come from? Did they just originate from life experiences and continue to develop? On the contrary, they were usually put forward in religious teachings and backed by warnings to the believers of punishment for transgressors.

Any society needs to agree upon a moral code, backed by a legal system to enforce it. A social system accepts the rules so that society can survive and evolve. Even in this age of impending globalization, some countries are ahead of others in the application of justice, whilst others have left behind the early applications of justice upheld by scripture and instead have pursued man-made interpretations, often influenced by politics. According to the Bahá'í teachings the twin pillars of justice are reward and punishment, as Bahá'u'lláh writes:

> Justice and equity are twin Guardians that watch over men. From them are revealed such blessed and perspicuous words as are the cause of the well-being of the world and the protection of the nations.[13]

Although Dawkins disposes quite eloquently of the claim that the religions have provided laws and moral guidance, it is quite plain from the study of the various religions that enshrined in their teachings are moral laws that were to suit the age and beyond, together with spiritual laws for eternity.

It is interesting that the attacks by the New Atheists have caused many religious people to re-examine their faith and in many cases has strengthened their resolve. Although it is sad that some have retaliated by blindly attacking evolutionary theory instead of studying it, quite a few have come to realize that stripping away the superstitions that had enveloped religious thought over the centuries is no bad thing. Ancient myths and teachings were in line with the comprehension of the time. Although myth and symbolism are mutual partners as we progress, unfortunately some people still like to hang on to the early literal explanations. We have to understand 'belief' and the confidence that is placed upon it by those who may not have studied the system that they have placed their trust in but who nevertheless have an ineluctable commitment to what they hold dear in their religion. Writer William Sears eloquently puts into context how many traditional Christians view unbelief:

> There are 'false prophets' who deceive many of the 'elect' in every age. These false prophets do not always appear in the guise of religion. There is the 'false prophet' who teaches that there is no God at all – atheism. The coming of this last 'false prophet', disbelief in God, was plainly foretold in both the Old and the New Testament for the 'time of the end'.[14]

The big problem for atheists in their attempts to debunk God is that God is unknowable, beyond our understanding, so we have the paradox of trying to disprove something that we cannot even envisage in the first place. We cannot comprehend a Creator who could set in motion the incredible universe; we have to revert to mere words. It is either vanity or curiosity that causes many to try to visualize God. But how is it possible? An atheist will condemn primitive imagery, but that is what humanity could contain within the mental capacity or conceptualization of the time.

We have progressed in our understanding of many things and cast aside much of our previous learning to produce new concepts, yet we remain in awe:

> If the veil were lifted, and the full glory of the station of those that have turned wholly towards God, and have, in their love for Him, renounced the world, were made manifest, the entire creation would be dumbfounded.[15]

Just as the evolution of thought has given us a greater understanding of natural processes, so true religion has always influenced civilization. Religious teachings, revealed in stages and constantly renewed or added to, have nurtured human civilization: nature and nurture working together. Not the free will that may be attributed to animals (freedom without purpose)

but the free will that should be nurtured or encouraged by religious teachings to 'hone' our spiritual development. Of course,
the gradual approach favoured by natural selection is extremely
logical and appealing to atheists because the logic is employed
to dispose of the existence of God, but it also underlines the
fact that we are trying to visualize God using an analysis based
upon our finite minds. We simply cannot envisage a Being that
could create the universe – or multiple universes, as postulated
by some. We have problems giving a name to this unknowable
Force. The wisdom of the Old Testament prophets in refusing
to use a name is thus apparent, but we are, however, given clues;
we can 'know' God through His Manifestations.

It is unfortunate that in this arena the views of atheists and
theists are poles apart. In view of the godlessness that now permeates society and the rejection of moral standards by many
of our young people, the attacks by Dawkins and others on
religious traditions and beliefs are quite timely. They appeal
to those who have rejected religious teachings together with
the moral guidance they offer and any form of law that might
inhibit their demands for freedom from restraint of any kind.
Yet the clash of religion and science has also made some think
a little more seriously about religion and enabled them to sort
the 'wheat from the chaff' in their search for the truth. There
is also the limitation of language; Dawkins' strong polemical
style and tone sells well. In some respects he could almost be
considered a priest for atheism.

Both religion and atheism then become casualties of
passion. When and wherever a religion dominates the lives
and minds of the populace, polemic is tightly controlled
and any attempt at discussion other than by the hierarchy is
ruthlessly suppressed. Stephen Phelps, a cosmologist, takes a
common-sense view:

> In a world threatened by religious extremism, the need to
> take stock in religion and to search for new perspectives is an

urgent one. Among the most vigorous of such examinations is a movement dubbed 'the new atheism,' led by scientists who argue that not only can science better explain reality than a belief in God but also that religious belief itself has become a threat to humanity. Foremost among this group is Richard Dawkins, a British ethologist and evolutionary biologist at Oxford University, whose latest book, *The God Delusion*, has remained near the top of best-seller lists.

"Faith can be very, very dangerous," writes Dr Dawkins. "Suicide bombers do what they do because they really believe what they were taught in their religious schools: that duty to God exceeds all other priorities . . .'

There are shades of meaning to the word faith. Faith has helped people to cope with suffering (mental and physical) and faith in medicine or even meditation, has often played a part.

But while Dr Dawkins and other new atheists believe the way forward lies in a world without religion, Bahá'ís approach the issue of God, nature, and religion from an entirely different perspective.

Stating that traditional religious beliefs are inadequate for the modern age, the Bahá'í Faith recasts the whole conception of religion, suggesting it is the principal force impelling the development of consciousness.

In this light, there is much in Dr Dawkins' book that Bahá'ís would agree with – including his condemnation of religious fanaticism, his call for the application of reason and science in the battle against irrational theologies, and his argument that the theory of evolution can explain the emergence of complex life.[16]

In *The Clash of Civilizations and the Remaking of World Order*, Professor Samuel Huntington comes to the following conclusion – which has been ignored by almost every reviewer of his book:

. . . as many have pointed out, whatever the degree to which they divided humankind, the world's major religions – Western Christianity Orthodoxy, Hinduism, Buddhism, Islam, Confucianism, Taoism, Judaism – also share key values in common. If humans are ever to develop a universal civilization, it will emerge gradually through the exploration and expansion of these commonalities.[17]

These commonalities are highlighted in the text entitled *One Common Faith*, issued by the Bahá'í World Centre in 2005 under the supervision of the Universal House of Justice, the governing body of the Bahá'í community. This introduces reviews and relevant passages from both the writings of Bahá'u'lláh and the scriptures of other faiths against the background of what is a contemporary crisis. *One Common Faith* argues that religion has been ignored by so many young people, who now turn to science for explanations, and it has been apparent for some time that religion in general has failed to keep up with such developments and explanations in line with new discoveries. In effect, God has been set aside and so-called atheists have rushed in to fill the vacuum that has ensued.

Another look at evolution and the ascent of man

Nevertheless, it may be that the origin of life is not the only major gap in the evolutionary story that is bridged by sheer luck, anthropically justified. For example, my colleague Mark Ridley in *Mendel's Demon* has suggested that the origin of the eukaryotic cell (our kind of cell with a nucleus and various other complicated features such as mitochondria, which are not present in bacteria) was an even more momentous, difficult and statistically improbable step than the origin of life. The origin of consciousness might be another major gap whose bridging was of the same order of improbability.[18]

Sheer luck, as in this passage from *The God Delusion*, seems to be acceptable for Dawkins and his supporters but would be ridiculed if claimed by those who believe that God was the Cause. Dawkins and many others with the same agenda have a comparatively easy task because they are literally pouring their ideas into a mental and spiritual void. This spiritual void is apparent in many people who have lost interest in religion, and when there is a strong reaction to the established belief systems, some are drawn to alternative (pseudo) religious ideas. The mainstream religions often do not know how to combat this. This leaves people wide open to atheistic arguments; many of those seeking answers to the question of our origins have little or no resistance that could stand up to the persuasive arguments of atheist 'experts' who maintain that everything in the universe 'happened' without any input from a Creator and that life as we know it probably evolved from a primordial soup.

When debating with Creationists (or perhaps it is more honest to say, attacking Creationists), atheists are bolstered by their belief in the evolutionary theory. The fall-back position for Creationists is usually the Bible and the limited description therein of how God created the world. With very little evidence as to where and when the Creation story originated, as opposed to the voluminous studies of Darwin and modern archaeology, it appears to be a very one-sided battle. The additional weakness of the Creationists lies in the fact that they argue amongst themselves as to the true meaning of the writings at their disposal. What were probably intended to be symbolic explanations for a primitive people have become accepted facts for modern Creationists. A simple re-think by both sides would perhaps enable them to accept that an unknowable Creator had set in motion the whole process, and in the fullness of time, when humanity had appeared and was ready, introduced a succession of prophets to enlighten and guide humanity.

Opponents of religious belief point to the creation stories as being unrealistic, ignoring the fact that such explanations were perfectly adequate for the age in which they were first revealed but failed to keep up with advances in knowledge. Change was often resisted by the religious leaders who felt threatened by new ideas, so for too long we have been conditioned to accept certain thoughts and ideas about how and why humanity was created. Religious extremists have retreated into banal explanations that would not satisfy a child who has been exposed to scientific evidence. Of course there are also different explanations between religions and sometimes even within a particular religion, a situation that has often led to schism and extremism. Conversely, atheism places its faith in a view of evolution that is strong but not actually conclusive. In fact, many scientific theories are also prone to that. Religion has a similar problem and relies heavily upon interpretations of scripture that are sometimes troublesome but could well be explained when religion is 'renewed' by the appearance of another Prophet or Messenger. In the terminology of the Bahá'í Faith, this is called *progressive revelation*, a concept that requires further investigation, and will be explored in another essay. It is linked with the Bahá'í view of evolution, both physical and spiritual, as Gary Matthews writes:

Thus Bahá'u'lláh strongly supports the biologist who finds for life a history stretching back through long but orderly stages of development. However, His teachings reject certain assumptions normally associated with this view. For one thing, Bahá'ís – unlike materialists – see nothing 'blind' about evolution. From start to finish, the process represents a gradual but resistless working out of God's purpose. Even though each step, viewed individually, may appear automatic or even random, the process as a whole is one of deliberate design.[19]

The Bahá'í teachings use the following analogy to describe the ascent of humanity and the purpose of our physical existence. In the womb we develop the senses and physical tools that we will need to lead a normal life. Once we are born, and as we grow physically and mentally, we also have the opportunity to grow spiritually, in preparation for the next stage or stages in an everlasting journey in the spiritual realms. Our physical existence is an opportunity to learn; to hone our spiritual qualities. The analogy of a baby in the womb is a useful way of explaining the true meaning of our existence. We are in the condition of babes in the womb; the baby does not understand why it has eyes, ears, etc. It has no use for them there, but when it leaves the womb and is born into this world, these faculties will enable it to function. So through the revealed laws of our God, we gain spiritual features or powers, as it were, of which we shall understand the real use after leaving the body.

Such a belief is anathema to atheists, but their own claims can be pompous, often impenetrable, as they struggle to explain the purpose of life and attempt to dispose of beliefs that are beyond their comprehension (even though respectable scientific discourse allows for many things being beyond our understanding). 'Abdu'l-Bahá made some interesting comments on the state of the theory of evolution around a hundred years ago, in 1912:

The philosophers of the Orient in reply to those of the western world say: Let us suppose that the human anatomy was primordially different from its present form, that it was gradually transformed from one stage to another until it attained its present likeness, that at one time it was similar to a fish, later an invertebrate and finally human. This anatomical evolution or progression does not alter or affect the statement that the development of man was always human in type and biological in progression. For the human embryo when examined microscopically is at first a mere germ or worm. Gradually as it develops it shows certain divisions; rudiments of hands and feet appear – that is to say, an upper and a lower part are distinguishable. Afterward it undergoes certain distinct changes until it reaches its actual human form and is born into this world. But at all times, even when the embryo resembled a worm, it was human in potentiality and character, not animal. The forms assumed by the human embryo in its successive changes do not prove that it is animal in its essential character. Throughout this progression there has been a transference of type, a conservation of species or kind. Realizing this we may acknowledge the fact that at one time man was an inmate of the sea, at another period an invertebrate, then a vertebrate and finally a human being standing erect. Though we admit these changes, we cannot say man is an animal. In each one of these stages are signs and evidences of his human existence and destination. Proof of this lies in the fact that in the embryo man still resembles a worm. This embryo still progresses from one state to another, assuming different forms until that which was potential in it -- namely, the human image – appears. Therefore, in the protoplasm, man is man. Conservation of species demands it.[20]

A naturalist attempts to go back through history, using the evidence provided by fossils, in order to promote the theory that all life can be shown to have been transitional. Yet there are no reliable transitional fossils. The British Museum of Natural History boasts the largest collection of fossils in the world. As far as is known, there is not one example of a transitional fossil. Charles Darwin wrote:

Lastly, looking not to any one time, but to all time, if my theory be true, numberless intermediate varieties, linking closely together all the species of the same group, must assuredly have existed. But, as by this theory, innumerable transitional forms must have existed, why do we not find them embedded in countless numbers in the crust of the earth? [21]

Although atheists delight in pointing out the errors of creationist arguments, they do not make allowances for the fact that these believers fervently believe that the Bible is based upon the Word of God. Some will aver that it has been preserved without error, and will not accept that there is a lot of symbolism and hidden meaning. 'Let the dead bury the dead' is an example of a symbolic truth misunderstood by Creationists and atheists alike. Probably the strongest argument against Creationism is that with the time scale that most of them accept, based upon the literal acceptance of the Genesis record, there has not been enough time for the different species to form and therefore they have to assume that no species have ever changed. Why can't they see that it is quite logical to accept that evolution is proof that God exists, and that Genesis is a symbolic story?

On the other hand, we have the intelligent design theory postulating that complex information (such as life on earth) requires an intelligent cause that should be detectable in some way. There are other arguments put forward, of which the Anthropic Principle is the most easily understood and is mirrored in the explanations of 'Abdu'l-Bahá:

> One of the proofs and demonstrations of the existence of God is the fact that man did not create himself: nay, his creator and designer is another than himself. [22]

Whatever the initial creation scenario was, and whatever our ancestors were like, we now differ considerably from animals; our teeth are not designed for tearing flesh, and we have the gift of speech. In addition we imbibe altruism, sympathy, empathy, remorse and sacrifice, all of which set us apart in evolutionary terms. Also, we continually question what goes on in the world, and that is the essence of our humanity.

The animal cannot understand the roundness of the earth, nor its motion in space, nor the central position of the sun, nor can it imagine such a thing as the all-pervading ether.[23]

Another vital difference, as described by Bahá'u'lláh, is that:

Arts, crafts and sciences uplift the world of being, and are conducive to its exaltation. Knowledge is as wings to man's life, and a ladder for his ascent. Its acquisition is incumbent upon everyone. The knowledge of such sciences, however, should be acquired as can profit the peoples of the earth, and not those which begin with words and end with words . . . knowledge is a veritable treasure for man, and a source of glory, of bounty, of joy, of exaltation, of cheer and gladness unto him. Happy the man that cleaveth unto it, and woe betide the heedless.[24]

Many scientists and anthropologists also claim that we are 'hard-wired' to believe in God or in 'gods'. This is natural because we cannot fully comprehend how creation came about or appreciate the immensity of the universe, so we are susceptible to 'supernatural' explanations. In this respect, many people either have a superstitious view that involves a supernatural being (often in human form) that is constantly intervening in human affairs with rewards and punishments; or alternatively, they misinterpret religious teachings in a way that causes them to reject belief in God. This group may call themselves atheist and prefer to postulate a view of evolution originating from a 'primeval soup' that eventually led to our present stage of existence. Those who subscribe to this have to leave ethics and jurisprudence for society and governments to resolve; in the ensuing mental and spiritual void that has been contaminating modern life an atheistic concept easily takes root.

On the other hand, there is sometimes a display of prejudice and paranoia amongst scientists when challenged by evidence that supports religious belief but does not seem to agree with scientific theory.

Different individuals may interpret facts in different ways, but that doesn't change the facts themselves. Theories may be good or bad in that they may be well established by factual evidence, or they may lack credibility. Before a theory is given any credence in our modern scientific community, it must be subjected to 'peer review'. This usually means that the proposed theory must be published in a legitimate scientific journal in order to provide the opportunity for other scientists to evaluate the relevant factual information and publish their conclusions.

As used in science, a theory is an explanation or model based on observation, experimentation and reasoning, especially one that has been tested and confirmed as a general principle helping to explain and predict natural phenomena. With the evidence so far, the theory of evolution answers more about the development of life on earth than the stories that are articulated by traditional religious teachers. Inevitably, both sides fall into the trap of quoting their viewpoints as conclusive in what has become a battle of words. Yet, as we have mentioned before but cannot reiterate enough, the 'potted histories' of religion contain a great deal of information that has been shrouded in a form that was easy to pass on and remember.

In the 18th and 19th centuries several new philosophies took root. The power of the word, the clash of wills and the different schools of thought, pondering the new avenues of knowledge that were opening up, promised to release humanity from the shackles of history and the power of established religions. Some were able to push the boundaries and realize what was needed, but others were restricted by the societies they lived in. All were affected by the 'spirit of the age' that spawned many new and conflicting ideas but no convincing answers, as Marzieh Gail describes:

> Our thousand schools of thought, offshoots of religious belief, are equally unable to bring men together. Philosophy cannot be lived without religion. Agnosticism will not satisfy an active mind. Atheism expounded is nothing less than theism with some changes of vocabulary, and the atheist is also groping for a standard.[25]

Fundamentalists, who prefer to accept one of the two versions of creation outlined in Genesis, cannot really provide a sensible argument because they rely upon a literal interpretation that is not supported by science or analysis. The fundamentalist position simply does not explain how the physical laws came into existence; it opposes the viewpoints of physicists without being able to provide alternative arguments. It relies wholly upon blind 'belief', refusing to consider that the writings relied upon may be symbolic or allegorical.

Nor do creationists usually tolerate alternative viewpoints, preferring to claim that the scriptural references they use are immutable. Many such Christians, and also many teachers of Islamic, Judaic, Buddhist or Hindu beliefs, cannot really consider anything that appears contrary to their interpretations (hence the many sects) and cannot easily be persuaded that perhaps they might have misunderstood any of their interpretations of holy writ. The battle lines are thus drawn; all sides in the argument avoiding compromise or consultation.

The challenge

In the continuing conflict between science and religion, Richard Dawkins has made the sweeping claim that God is unnecessary and science can explain nature without any help from supernatural forces like God. In his view there is no need for a Creator. But surely, as nature is also a part of our existence, whatever the explanation about how it evolved; it was created in some way? We have noted that the legends and myths of religious history usually have a hidden reality – the events they refer to may well have happened, but not necessarily as we understand them.

Often it is a matter of finding the right words (even though it is impossible to contain the Creator in mere words and the spiritual aspects are often missed). It has already been pointed out that understanding the concept of a Creator is difficult – who can really define existence and non-existence outside of our own experience? We may have to use figurative language to even explain what we mean when we refer to a Creator, so in this respect there is lot to be said for pure faith and trust. A believer will trust that the essence of his religion contains a spiritual message for humanity that came from a divine source, in much the same way that a scientist believes that the essence of his work stems from the immutable physical rules that underlie the physical world.

Some atheists trust that science will eventually provide most of the answers to explain our existence but find the concept of God impossible to accept. They therefore refuse to investigate the inner, subtle teachings of the scriptures in order to come to an understanding of what inspires a believer; for whom spiritual energy may be transmuted into action, as with the fabric of the universe where energy is transmuted into form. Atheists and theists (using the terms collectively) are therefore constantly confronting each other with their 'proofs' rather than attempting dialogue and seeking common ground.

The image of God that is obtained from a simple acceptance of the story in Genesis, for example, is not sufficient for educated people but was quite sufficient for our distant ancestors who delighted in the imagery. In this age we are surely able to understand that God isn't a person, even though some still prefer to think that way, and this invites ridicule from committed atheists such as Dawkins who have an agenda to adhere to. In fact, God has never actually been put forward as a *person* in any of the major religions, but use has been made of images to present, in the form of artistic symbols, a representation of something that they are unable to explain in any other way. A similar problem arises with the station of the Prophets or Messengers. 'Abdu'l-Bahá gives this example:

> . . . whoso looketh for Christ in His physical body hath looked in vain, and will be shut away from Him as by a veil. But whoso yearneth to find Him in the spirit will grow from day to day in joy and desire and burning love, in closeness to Him, and in beholding Him clear and plain.[26]

Unfortunately, with all major religions of the past explanations had to be in accordance with the interpretations of those who claimed authority, and this led to conflicting opinions and schism. For example, the writings attributed to the disciples of Christ actually have a reduced claim to authenticity simply because they were not written down for a generation or more after the death of Christ and it is in those writings that Jesus is transformed from being a spokesman for God, a channel or Messenger, to being the *physical* Son of God. This is despite some of His words being quite clear about His station. In fact, some go much further in claiming that His mother, Mary was taken bodily into heaven in the event known as the Assumption.

At present there is a greater awareness of the gulf between creation as taught by fundamentalist groups and creation according to the theories put forward by Darwinism and natural selection, and there is no doubt that it causes harmful rifts. Supporters of the opposing camps make demeaning statements about each other that are designed to make the claims seem too extreme to warrant support. So, the Creationists are accused of believing that the world is around 6,000 years old and the Darwinists (if we may use the term collectively) are said to believe that natural selection through an evolutionary process is the only possible answer. This adversarial stance hampers any possibility of investigation into a middle way. In reality, each of the supposed camps are the outer fringes of dialectical discussion that seek constantly to find evidence to support their own theories. This surely leaves ample room for schools of thought that are ready and willing to consider all options and to allow for the possibility that new evidence will be forthcoming; that there is in fact an alternative understanding.

The crux of the matter is that many scientists cannot accept the idea of a God or Creator and many Creationists will not allow for anything that does not fit their interpretations of scripture. Even if you underwrite the 'Big Bang' theory you are still presented with a creative process rather than an accidental one, and Darwinian evolution is also a creative process. Darwinists used to seize upon the fact that some apes can learn to crack a nut with a heavy stone or use a twig as a tool as evidence that humans were descended from them. But in that case, where did apes go wrong? – if (as is believed) we merely *split* in evolutionary terms? So the modern suggestion is that the apes were a branch from a common ancestor. The tools acquired by apes came via experience that may or may not be passed on to future generations; and wondering about the reasons for their existence and the meaning of life is (as far as we know) alien to them. The creativity, curiosity and propensity of humans to acquire knowledge is far beyond that of apes, as 'Abdu'l-Bahá describes:

> One of the strangest things witnessed is that the materialists of today are proud of their natural instincts and bondage. They state that nothing is entitled to belief and acceptance except that which is sensible or tangible. By their own statements they are captives of nature, unconscious of the spiritual

world, uninformed of the divine Kingdom and unaware of heavenly bestowals. If this be a virtue, the animal has attained it to a superlative degree, for the animal is absolutely ignorant of the realm of spirit and out of touch with the inner world of conscious realization. The animal would agree with the materialist in denying the existence of that which transcends the senses. If we admit that being limited to the plane of the senses is a virtue, the animal is indeed more virtuous than man, for it is entirely bereft of that which lies beyond, absolutely oblivious of the kingdom of God and its traces whereas God has deposited within the human creature an illimitable power by which he can rule the world of nature.[27]

But even according to the view that sees apes and humans as descended from a common ancestor, the split from some ancient lineage caused us to evolve along a path that gave us greater powers, setting us apart from the rest of creation and allowing us to philosophize on the meaning of life and perhaps appreciate that we were not only created, but created for a purpose. Could any in the animal kingdom have achieved such a level of awareness? It sets us apart. The purpose and meaning of life is answered by religion; by the profound teachings of religious innovators, the founders of the major religions who sought to instill into humanity a unity of purpose that would impel us forward to a unique state of being forever beyond anything that the other forms of life could ever reach. The question that we often hear, *what is the meaning of life?* may be answered by this statement made as part of a prayer, not too difficult for humans to understand and providing an explanation that atheists surely cannot match: 'I bear witness, O My God, that Thou hast created me to know Thee and to worship Thee.'[28]

So the defining moments for the human race have been the appearance of the major religions. All religions start from within a certain mindset, and the teachings then influence a move away from the traditional ideas and help kick-start the renewal of society by injecting fresh teachings and ideas that are always needed for progress. Above all, religion preaches peace and unity, although that still seems a distant dream. For in the words of Abraham Lincoln in his address to Congress in 1862, 'The dogmas of the quiet past are inadequate for the stormy present.'

Nevertheless, certain spiritual teachings are for all time, which has prompted some to say that the teachings of Christ were not new. The teachings that are changeable, because of changing conditions, are the social or dietary laws, and it is mainly these that caused initial antagonism towards a new revelation.

We also have to allow that everyone has a right to believe or not believe. The Qur'án tells us, 'There is no compulsion in religion.' [29] Yet despite this clear teaching, many Muslims are quite rigid in their interpretation of what they term apostasy and the punishment is often death. The UN Declaration of Human Rights states: 'Everyone has the right to freedom of thought, conscience and religion; this right includes freedom to change his religion or belief . . .'[30] Most countries have signed up to this, but many find ways to ignore it.

Human beings murder, torture and in many ways provide all manner of affliction for fellow human beings and provide all manner of excuses to justify it. Yet they may also be tormented by guilt and seek to provide a reason. This is conscience, another attribute that sets us apart from the animal kingdom.

The complexity of life forms and the immensity of space cannot be fully explained or understood, and we have established that any conception of a Creator responsible for all this cannot be envisaged by human intellect, no matter how abstract the ideas that may be put forward. The challenge is to give credence to the belief that a divine plan exists, as in the words that Shakespeare gave to Hamlet: 'There's a divinity that shapes our ends, Rough-hew them how we will.' [31]

4

The Evolution of Spirituality

With regard to the problem of the 'meaning' of life and the battle to find certain words to convey this to different generations, it has to be understood that not only do meanings evolve as we become more knowledgeable but that this process is essential for a 'renewal of civilization' that will eventually involve all nations. Consider for example *spirituality*. My personal understanding is this (and it does not quite equate with the dictionary): that it is an attitude of mind or personality that manifests itself in the form of humility and self-effacement in service to a cause or belief that is beyond normal human values or existence. Why do I feel that I can propose a new meaning for a word such as this? Because I feel that in this age all has been renewed, and the renewal of civilization and religion extends to the regeneration of words and their meanings. Observation of those meanings is the key.

The powerful force that came with a belief in the importance of the *individual* emanated from the teachings of Buddha, and the virtues of self-reliance and personal independence led eventually to Christ's teachings for the individual, the logical next step in a spiritual chain of events. Self-effacement, keeping oneself in the background in a controlled manner, is an example of self-control that would be necessary for a true expression of the individualism that came with Buddhism – in other words, humility or a lack of false pride that could come from the confidence inspired by realization of the true self.

It is interesting to think about the evolution of spiritual

consciousness and the exercise of free will that may eventually lead towards planetary unity. Science should one day lead us along a path to material prosperity that could harmonize with spiritual development lead to the consciousness of 'one planet, one people'. But the process starts with religion. Science can neither bring about a change of consciousness nor discern new standards of value, let alone set absolute standards. It is the revealed religions that have always succeeded in effecting a change in man. Each one of them has brought about such a change and produced a new type of man, has reorientated the life of the community towards new goals and values, thereby overcoming what had been undermining society; namely, antagonistic thinking on the central questions of life, the pluralism of uncommitted opinions and the non-obligatory character of all norms and goals. Udo Schaefer writes:

> In Scripture we frequently come across the allegory of the divine physician who, in his superior wisdom, examines the ailing body of mankind, diagnoses its sickness and prescribes the appropriate remedy. Thus, salvation is offered not only to the individual grace-seeking soul but also to the collective, **to the entire human race.** [1]

Religion is usually attacked by atheists on the grounds that many of its traditions are outdated or superstitious. In response, proof or *creation evidence* (whatever that means) is constantly sought by Creationists to discredit evolution, but in doing so they dig themselves into a hole. For example, the Bible does not actually state that the earth is just a few thousand years old; this is the interpretation of some theologians and Bible 'experts'. As we have seen, all the religions use symbolism in their scriptures, and sometimes they have both a literal and a symbolic meaning, as Robert McLaughlin points out:

When phenomena, such as earthquakes or the appearance of stars, are mentioned in the Scriptures, they may be understood literally, or symbolically, or in both senses.[2]

To be fair, when we say that many scientists do not believe in God we overlook the important fact that they do not believe in the god that is bounded by the limitations of the human mind, and resent having to admit that a supreme Creator is impossible to comprehend through the senses. Being scientists, they seek proof. Unfortunately, their investigations are hampered by their inability to probe the metaphysical in a way that would satisfy them. Words and theories cannot encompass the Creator without recourse to metaphors and poetic images.

Most science courses today include studies in evolution, although there is still strong resistance in some quarters; the most extreme examples being the Creationist movements that have a strong following in the United States. This does not bode well for bringing science and religion together in harmony. Both sides will have to re-adjust.

In its infancy, modern science went through a long process of opposition from powerful religious authorities based on ignorance and superstition, although it blossomed under Islam in its more enlightened period of growth. Many of the early scientists and inventors often chose to be known as 'alchemists' to avoid being accused of witchcraft, disguising what they were doing because of superstition and suspicion from the opponents of new ideas.

There are always disagreements among scientists, just as there are amongst religious sects, but usually in countries where freedom of thought is allowed without persecution. But professionalism has a tendency to create 'ivory towers'. In medicine, for example, the attitude towards patients has undergone a sea-change in recent years – at least in some countries – with practitioners being bound to explain and treat patients on a more equal level, rather than being unwelcoming to criticism. Psychiatry is also a case in point, where some patients are left on medication for years because of a blanket diagnosis that is applied to multiple cases that could be open to question if investigated more thoroughly.

Informed debate and true consultation need to replace the arrogance that often distorts science just as much as it distorts religion. Research in all fields of science and religion should always be ongoing and encouraged, otherwise progress is inhibited. However, one danger in traditional religion is that the teachings were for centuries often reinforced by anecdotes, symbolism and traditions as explained by teachers/priests/clerics to believers who did not always have the ability or desire to fully investigate for themselves. We have to accept that this was in keeping with the imperfect knowledge of the age, and that many of those ideas have since been re-evaluated as science and religious knowledge have gained new insights through research and devised new ways of investigating the evidence.

In contrast to the past, people are now more willing to accept new scientific discoveries and are becoming less tolerant what religious people believe and teach. There is resistance from both sides, because those who have gained power and social prestige through religion are reluctant to change as social circumstances alter. It is also true, as the New Atheists have been quick to point out, that religion has also carried out many atrocities in the name of 'faith' at various times in history; most people have heard of the excesses carried out during the Crusades and the Inquisition. Priests and other religious authorities in any faith gain prestige and power through their work and do not easily relinquish it. Their 'flock' are indoctrinated into believing that only they have access to the truth (the only truth) and other 'experts' or religious organizations are flawed and in error. The worst-case scenario is when some of the extremist groups advise their followers not to even investigate other faiths or scientific research because the 'devil' will use this to lead them into error.

As mentioned above, the social rules that have been adopted by different faiths naturally become outmoded over a long period of time, but in some instances they are practised with such fervour that it becomes accepted as 'sinful' not to heed them. An extreme example is the Orthodox Jewish interpretation of work on the Sabbath, where switching on a light or pressing a button in a lift is considered work and is forbidden. Natural progress in civilized society makes such teachings obsolete. Also, shades of meaning as between different sects have caused lasting divisions.

Certain prohibitions obviously made sense at the time they were first revealed, but such laws imposed by religious teachings were for the protection of society and the progress of humanity at the time of revelation. If the religion was accepted by the people then those rules became binding. But progress means that society would eventually change, so certain laws would also need to change. One example is 'an eye for an eye, and a tooth for a tooth',[3] which was acceptable at a certain stage in our evolution because it sent a powerful signal that certain actions were not acceptable and would be punished in the same way as the violation; whilst the laws outlined in Leviticus are even more unsuitable for modern life.

Even though in most countries there is now segregation of church and state, the laws are generally in line with the main teachings of the state religion. This has led to a 'war of values':

Moral and social law can for the first time in human experience blend and unify when humanity as a whole becomes subject to the same law. Everything universal is divine truth; everything limited and partisan is human opinion. The obligation and right to live in a moral society has become crucial, a test of our will to survive. The modern struggle which employs nations as its instruments is not a war of peoples nor of dynasties: it is a war of values. The dispute about values resolves itself into a struggle between those human beings who would and must unite in a common humanity and a common social body, and those who would and must remain separate, diverse and autonomous. The national state is itself torn and divided in a struggle which involves primarily the conscious attitudes of individual human beings. But to the degree that the national state can act as a united body, it is unable to avoid participation in the decision. No person and no social body is immune from destiny. The true destiny of the national state is to build the bridge from local autonomy to world unity. [4]

It is unfortunate that in modern society, both inside and outside of religious groups, people seem to have lost their way, floundering in a no-man's-land of confused ideals and anti-social norms. Yet religion can still inspire and motivate. Followers expect good moral guidance but are often frustrated by human weakness and an irresponsible or misguided rendition, often leading to extremism of one sort or another.

We have to accept that material progress is unstoppable, although it can be interrupted by war or natural disasters. Evolutionary progress is the same, and future evolutionary progress will be linked to advances in consciousness and spirituality.

For too long we have been steeped in superstition and unbelief because of the distorted messages that have been passed down to us by those who claim to understand the message of the prophets.

It is a fact that records from ancient history were not preserved meticulously as archival material and then conveyed to the masses, but as something that had for a long time been retained in the memory of society and often embellished with romantic notions or exaggerations that the people liked to hear. But present-day critics of ancient records or religious literature replace critical analysis with rather insensitive ridicule. This ignores the core message.

A further problem is that religious extremists will even argue over what and how to wear certain items that they link with their beliefs; how and when to pray; the role of women; what constitutes apostasy and what should be the punishment (if any) for it. The sacredness of life and the full meaning of the teachings are lost in a plethora of man-made customs and traditions; subjugated to ritual and losing sight of spirituality and inner meanings. It is because of these errors that the accusation of superstitious nonsense is thrown at all religious belief by those who wish to denigrate religion. It completely ignores the beauty, comfort, support and meaning that religion has given to millions.

Religion and spirituality still play an important role in the lives of the majority of human beings; they are essential to their well-being. Nevertheless, the signs are everywhere that society is struggling to cope with the loss of certain values that they identified with their beliefs. Ian Angell writes:

> The reason why we in the West are so mired in moral relativism is that the common values and rituals of the status quo no longer glue our society together. Many in our society are experimenting with alternatives; and new communication technologies make it so very much easier to find out about other communities, other moralities, and then to compare and contrast their relative merits. With this new-found knowledge, individuals are pulling away from their old communities and pulling apart their old moralities.[5]

The failure in the banking system in 2008/9 that rocked the finances of several major countries and is still with us today was caused primarily by the abandonment of ethical guidelines in the pursuit of profit. The success or failure of the modern phenomena of globalization is itself greatly dependent upon eventual world unity and a sound approach to ethics in business and politics if it is to succeed. Undermining all the tentative attempts at world unity and peace is corruption; the enormity of this problem is currently defeating both governments and philosophers. There is surely no possibility for world unity, peace and prosperity without ethics. How do we deal with this? It will require drastic improvements in social behaviour and we will need to tackle family values as a starting point, but above all it would need guidance from a source that all could respect. Will it ultimately be religion or politics that will solve the problems that face society? If the task ultimately lies with government, it will need to be a government that respects moral law and religious ideals above political expediency. This is difficult, as Sun Libo points out:

> In the East, philosophers hoped that morality would continue to improve, eventually overcome human weakness, and nurture kind and just behaviour. In the West, philosophers attempted to incorporate justice into a form of order, and use the law to control the less desirable aspects of human nature so that the principle of justice could be manifested through the law.
>
> It has proven difficult to realise justice either through the enhancement of morality or the establishment of a social order. The power of morality alone, without a corresponding system, cannot establish a truly just society. Likewise, the establishment of a system alone will fail without the proper moral concepts. The best system requires the internal constraints of moral values, and its promulgation and authority must have the support of honesty, sacrifice and other individual virtues.[6]

In contrast, Dawkins suggests in *The God Delusion* that it is religion that is connected with higher crime rates – a classic example of how all sorts of conclusions can be read into crime and population statistics.[7] Fukuyama, author of *The End of History*, also highlights the 'desire for recognition' as a crucial factor in crime that manifests itself in many ways, pointing out that this is also linked with 'shame' as well as 'self-esteem'. None of these explanations of crime are conclusive. Amazingly, there are also desperate attempts to show that animals and insects practise altruism, rather than accept that humanity is a unique handiwork with a destiny and purpose.

The standards of ideal moral behaviour that are demanded of believers can be gleaned from a study of the teachings of the major religions and it can be seen that they evolve as society evolves, in the same way that the discipline placed upon a child changes as their understanding grows of right and wrong, and their ability to absorb those changes evolves. We do not explain all the laws of physics to a four-year-old because their comprehension, and adjusting to the world around them, is a gradual process. We find ways of introducing aspects of the physical world using metaphor and analogies; likewise with all education. In my pre-teen years I remember my science master dramatically driving home the functions of a capacitor that I was having difficulty comprehending, by dumping the contents of the wastebasket onto the floor and saying, 'capacitor discharging' ! Then scooping the rubbish back into the basket and saying 'capacitor charging'! Realization came and I was able to move on with my early understanding of electronics. The teaching example was simple, unexpected and credible, but not one that would be taught to a student of physics at university.

By comparison, Richard Dawkins' attempt to link accounts of miracles with the remote possibility that 'jiggling atoms' might just cause the arm of a statue to move and therefore not be a miracle, is a mere jibe;[8] it may be effective for some audiences but it is quite a juvenile attempt at ridicule. As modern cosmological studies have demonstrated, it is life on earth that is the true miracle.

Reconciling science and religion

We must endeavour to develop a form of reconciliation between the opposing interpretations of the meaning of life. Is there an answer that would satisfy?

The teachings of religion evolve from the appearance of a new revelation or prophet and the resistance to new teachings are often strong, due to vested interests in the old order and the fact that new ideas threaten the position and authority of the established hierarchy. This also happens in science when there is resistance to new discoveries and theories; Einstein's initial reaction to quantum mechanics is an example. And in 2010 Professor Francisco Ayala had this to say:

> Science and religion cannot be in contradiction because they address different questions. It is only when either subject oversteps its boundary, as he believes is the case with Professor Dawkins, that a contradiction arises . . . The scientific fundamentalism proposed by Dawkins implies a materialistic view of the world. But once science has had its say, there remains much about reality that is of interest. Common sense tells us that science can't tell us everything.[9]

Right from early history, when philosophers and scholars started to debate what religion and science had in common, it was realized that they were intertwined and each had a contribution to make that could explain life and the universe. 'Abdu'l-Bahá spoke of science as 'the first emanation from God':

> Science is the first emanation from God toward man. All created beings embody the potentiality of material perfection, but the power of intellectual investigation and scientific acquisition is a higher virtue specialized to man alone. Other beings and organisms are deprived of this potentiality and

attainment. God has created or deposited this love of reality in man. The development and progress of a nation is according to the measure and degree of that nation's scientific attainments. Through this means, its greatness is continually increased and day by day the welfare and prosperity of its people are assured.[10]

Some have claimed that science is based on absolute certainty, while ethics has no general basis at all. This is surely wrong on both points. Science works on the basis of experiments and/or experience and should be open to new ideas that may confirm or deny previous results. Scientists have often exhibited erratic behaviour and made claims that later prove to be erroneous, but the strength of the scientific method surely lies in the fact that later evidence can be accepted and facts reexamined. Science's weakness sometimes lies in the scramble for funds that may tempt scientists to fudge certain issues.

Religion is not really compatible with scientific analysis. Religious authorities find that being open to new ideas is difficult to do, and rather than accept changes to their beliefs will often break away into sects. For atheists, God is considered a projection of man's need for an omnipotent power to explain the mystery of the universe and creation; they reject the claim that ethics and morality originated from religious teaching and appeal to the higher consciousness that is innate in human beings.

It is perhaps more difficult for scientists than for others to declare their belief in God, because of their training in the scientific method. However, in the past and even today, many scientists believe that God exists and is responsible for what we see in nature. Dr Auguste Forel, a Swiss neuroanatomist and psychiatrist, accepted the teachings of Bahá'u'lláh after receiving a profound explanation from 'Abdu'l-Bahá of the existence of God. Among other things, 'Abdu'l-Bahá wrote:

As to the attributes and perfections such as will, knowledge, power and other ancient attributes that we ascribe to that Divine Reality, these are the signs that reflect the existence of beings in the visible plane and not the absolute perfections of the Divine Essence that cannot be comprehended. For instance, as we consider created things we observe infinite perfections, and the created things being in the utmost regularity and perfection we infer that the Ancient Power on whom dependeth the existence of these beings, cannot be ignorant; thus we say He is All-Knowing. It is certain that it is not impotent, it must be he All-Powerful; it is not poor, it must be All-Possessing; it is not non-existent, it must be Ever-Living. The purpose is to show that these attributes and perfections that we recount for that Universal Reality are only in order to deny imperfections, rather than to assert the perfections that the human mind can conceive. Thus we say His attributes are unknowable.[11]

We have seen that the harmony of religion and science has a high priority in the Bahá'í Faith. It might be thought that for such harmony to succeed there would have to be a situation where either or both gave way on certain points in order to achieve it. Some might think that this would lead to a 'watering down' of important issues. In fact, to quote from Roger Prentice, 'There would be no giving way because they are different aspects of human consciousness and truth-telling. Both are valid – but not in terms of each other.'[12]

   David Hofman describes the dependence of humanity on both religion and science:

Science does not oppose the moral precepts inculcated by religion, but it does occasionally recommend the adoption of new practices and the discontinuance of old ones, in order to promote the general welfare. But in general, science is confined to investigation and the production of facts, and it is up to the rest of humanity to make the best use of them. And it is here that religion plays its part; for upon the spiritual condition of mankind depend the uses to which scientific power is put, whether to the enrichment or the destruction of human life.[13]

Progressive revelation

Atheists claim that the religions are so diverse that they create a confusion of beliefs with no purposeful pattern. But those who believe in their religion, if they are observant, can also discern a pattern that links religions. If it can be seen that the central ideas have been repeated, with some evidence that such ideas have been progressively nudging humanity through stages of growth that were ever-advancing, then this surely fits the criteria for scientific analysis and is worthy of serious study. 'Abdu'l-Bahá said,

> We should earnestly seek and thoroughly investigate realities, recognizing that the purpose of the religion of God is the education of humanity and the unity and fellowship of mankind. Furthermore, we will establish the point that the foundations of the religions of God are one foundation.[14]

Progressive revelation is a Bahá'í teaching that encapsulates the idea of a creative process and links it with a divine plan that, through a study of history, may be seen in action. Throughout history, the teachings that were revealed by the Messengers of God (the founders of the great religions) have contained guidance for humanity. They stimulated spiritual and material growth amongst those who came under their influence and tried to put them into practice. If the power contained within the teachings promotes spiritual and material development, then society prospers and civilization advances. Through this very advancement, humanity matures and requires increased knowledge from the divine source. Unfortunately, if over a period of time people do not perceive an increase in such knowledge (perhaps because the majority have rejected the renewal of religion through a new Messenger), there is a gradual falling away as people neglect their beliefs. Problems arise; as society tries to adjust, it goes through a time of troubles.

In his mammoth work *A Study of History*, Arnold Toynbee drew attention to the *time of troubles* which followed the collapse of the Hellenic civilization and preceded the rise to greatness of the Roman Empire, repeating itself with the collapse of Roman civilization and the emergence of the Islamic Empire. The lesson from history is that if the teachings are accepted in their entirety and actions are controlled by the spiritual laws that come with the message; it augers well for an ever-advancing civilization. If it is rejected or only parts are accepted, then the power is not fully instilled into the culture; divisions then appear that lead to all manner of problems as society tries to adjust to dynamic change whilst riven with disunity. The following quotation from the talks of 'Abdu'l-Bahá refers to all the major religions, yet could equally apply to the early tribal societies, prior to Buddha's revelation.

When a movement fundamentally religious makes a weak nation strong, changes a nondescript tribal people into a mighty and powerful civilization, rescues them from captivity and elevates them to sovereignty, transforms their ignorance into knowledge and endows them with an impetus of advancement in all degrees of development (this is not theory, but historical fact) it becomes evident that religion is the cause of man's attainment to honour and sublimity. [15]

A tribe is a greatly extended community, a social division or kin group. In a tribal situation, providing there is discipline from the top (similar to the way dictatorial rulers maintain control) personal ambitions are kept in check through fear of being classed as an outsider or outcast. Those ambitions will still be there; perhaps stifled, but surfacing from time to time and threatening stability. In past tribal society there would have been ample opportunity for self-expression, but there would also have been limitations, simply because of the hierarchy and the possibility of an internal threat to the leadership. Of course, the interaction (assuming conditions within the society are relaxed enough to allow some self-expression) would inevitably lead to expression of self.

Constructive thinking only develops fully through free communication. This is a separate philosophical subject beyond the scope of this book, except to point out that it started to become more important in Jeremiah and in Zoroastrian commentaries. The essence of the major religions is monotheism, although this statement has to be tempered by the fact that at first glance, Buddhism and Hinduism do not appear to be monotheistic; a closer study reveals the reason for this. In Hinduism, there is strong emphasis on the *attributes* of a supreme Being that, over time, became misrepresented as minor deities and led to many errors, including a belief in reincarnation. This did not actually become a belief until well into the period covered by the Upanishads, which were discourses upon the Vedas.

Individuality seems to be a link between the teachings of Zoroaster, which greatly influenced Iranian culture. Zoroastrianism took hold in Persia around 800 BCE. Although the religion itself was hard-pressed to survive the onslaught of various invaders, the ideas persisted and permeated society and influenced a wide area of the ancient world, persisting through many generations. The underlying effect of the teachings on Iranian history was subtle and dealt with the responsibilities that would come with openly expressing individuality.

Zoroaster's influence on the tribalism that had hampered free will and individual action was a preparation for new patterns of development that would allow for the flowering of individuality, remembering of course that religious teachings are always revealed to assist and protect the whole of humanity and not just one group. A gradual preparation for the break from tribalism is expressed in the teachings of the Zend Avesta and the Gathas, and indeed in the Old Testament (Jeremiah). In both sources, taking responsibility for your own actions and service to the community are highly commended, together with charitable acts, good thoughts and good deeds. The Gathas proclaimed that we are free and responsible beings.

There has always been interaction between the various faiths. At times, under certain leaders, some debates have been allowed. In this way, as religious leaders sought to analyse and strengthen their own faith, they would inevitably influence each other to some degree. To counter previous deviations, the Buddha placed more emphasis on the central message of self-development and to no longer being attached to earthly things as the essential path to awareness and peace. Buddhism was founded in India circa 500 BCE and its influence spread throughout Asia and the Far East. There is great confusion amongst the various sects of Buddhism as to whether the Buddha taught anything substantive about a Creator/God because he laid so much emphasis upon self-awareness and because nothing was written down for several hundred years that could be reliably investigated.

It is often claimed that Buddhism is a religion that does not accept God in the sense that other faiths do. However, Mahatma Gandhi dealt with the suggestion that Buddha rejected the concept of God.

I have heard it contended times without number and I have read in books claiming to express the spirit of Buddhism, that the Buddha did not believe in God. In my humble opinion such a belief contradicts the very central fact of Buddha's teaching. Confusion has risen over His rejection, and just rejection, of the base things that passed in His generation under the name of God. He undoubtedly rejected the notion that a being called God could be actuated by malice, could repent of His actions, and like the kings of the earth could possibly be open to temptation and bribes and could have favourites.[16]

What came later (after Buddhism) was the acceptance among the Greeks that the *polis* (the city) required a sense of duty toward the state; according to Thucydides, 'it is the citizens who are the Polis'.

Although Christianity appeared around 2 BCE through the teachings of Jesus of Nazareth, it did not take hold as an organized religion for about 200 years, after a struggle between different groups was finally settled through the intervention of the Roman Emperor Constantine. Islam, based upon the teachings of Muhammad, took hold in Arabia in 622 AD. Soon after the death of Muhammad the first major split occurred in Islam, and other divisions came later.

All religions have eventually been rent by schism to varying degrees, because distorted interpretations obscured the real purpose of certain texts and superstitious practices were adopted that demean the true faith. The Christian Church sent devout fighters into battle carrying a cross, turning a symbol of peace and love into a symbol of war – not only during the medieval Crusades but in the 20th century. Its followers still argue about the definition of a 'just war'. The Muslim clergy sent innocent believers into battle against fellow Muslims in the Iran/Iraq war, carrying plastic keys that would 'guarantee' them a place in paradise. Ordinary people do not or cannot question such deliberate deceptions introduced by their leaders, yet in every such case the numbers of the faithful grow and give more power to the clerics.

The Bahá'í Faith is the most recent of the world religions, and despite terrible and continuing persecution in the land of its birth is now firmly established throughout the entire world. It has an extremely enlightened outlook that is compatible with the scientific advances of the modern world.

This quick trip through the major religions is merely to highlight the fact that each faith has connections with the others and has grown with and played its part in the progress of the human race, because the underlying purpose of each new religion has been to propel humanity onward. A deeper study will show that you can discern a pattern, a progressive development that despite opposition and setbacks has informed advances in society, and has been remarked upon by many notable historians.

The stepping stones or keys to spiritual evolution in any society, as outlined in this book, could never be completely eliminated by the mistakes of those who sought to distort the religion for their own ends. This must surely be because the underlying power of the central message was enshrined within the teachings and 'not one jot or tittle'[17] would be taken away. All scripture, despite the accretion of certain errors throughout the centuries, has its part to play in progressive revelation. It carries a spiritual message that has been to the ultimate benefit of the human race, despite human weakness and resistance.

The evidence of such a central message is plain to see. The divine plan has unfolded throughout history and provided guidance for the well-being of humankind; this claim can be investigated by an unprejudiced study of history. In science and evolutionary theory there should always be checks and balances, and a sensible review of later interpretations, and this should also apply to the teachings and claims of all the religions. As has been mentioned, each revelation provided a fresh impulse, through laws and teachings that were designed to propel society forward, and there were certain protective measures or guidance enshrined therein, although over the course of history these may have become blurred and in some instances changed to make them easier to understand.

There would be several reasons for this. Original documents for some aspects of the religion may not have existed, or too much reliance would be placed upon oral history and tradition. Some texts such as the Dead Sea Scrolls seem to corroborate portions of the Old Testament and there is constant research into all scripture, but the Qur'án was the first real example of undisputed scripture. The disputes in Islam have always been about interpretation and meaning, not about the validity of the Qur'án itself. Still, every religion has received its share of revelation, as Bahá'u'lláh affirms:

> . . . at one time We address the people of the Torah . . . At another, We address the people of the Evangel . . . At still another, We address the people of the Qur'án saying 'Fear the All-Merciful, and cavil not at Him through Whom all religions were founded' . . . Know thou moreover, that We have addressed to the Magians Our Tablets, and adorned them with Our Law . . . We have revealed in them the essence of all the hints and allusions contained in their Books. The Lord, verily, is the Almighty, the All-Knowing.[18]

Religious history is inseparable from social history and has bound communities together, although not always as intended, as we have seen from the internecine struggles often fomented by vested interests. However, Fukuyama in *Trust* spoke of the accumulation of 'social capital' as a force that creates strong communities, and as history (especially religious history) is a process of change, it is through this that we have come to understand the accumulation of social capital. It had previously been noted by eminent historians such as Karl Jaspers (1883–1969) and Arnold Toynbee (1889–1975) that prior to the inception of a new religion there was always a proliferation of ideas that appeared to be a preparation for the teachings that were about to be revealed to humanity, as though subjective knowledge and ideas were being filtered into the human psyche in readiness for what was to come, thus creating an air of expectancy and investigation from within society.

Of course, the old system does not immediately collapse and the new one rise in its stead. There is always a period of time when the two overlap and the enthusiasm for the new clashes with the defence of the old; and as we know, there is nearly always a resistance to change. Oswald Spengler (1880–1936) also felt that the history of cultures followed a similar pattern – that there is a spring, summer, autumn, winter, so the impact of social forces, influenced by religion, eventually dictates the direction society will take. Consciousness and progress develop through input from the environment, together with culture and experience, and religion has always played a vital part in this. Spiritual and religious progression can therefore be seen as inseparable from human development; if we don't understand history, we cannot understand the present. The analogy of a gradual unfolding of capacity can be observed in children, and equates well with the development of humanity as a whole.

Acquired knowledge is another matter. The power to learn or retain knowledge governs the level of knowledge that is able to be absorbed and how it is then utilized. The formative years in either the growth of the human child or the development of society require do's and don'ts so that we do not become anti-social. Physically and spiritually, we are like a slate upon which will be recorded the rewards and the pitfalls of our journey. In the words of Omar Khayyam: 'And the moving finger writes, and having writ, moves on . . .'

The unnecessary conflict

We have now entered the scientific age and are unlocking many secrets that were out of the reach of our ancestors. There is no doubt that this age has produced much that is of great material benefit, but at the same time humanity has witnessed a steep decline in religious belief as people have begun to question and reject many of the concepts that they had previously held to be true. In reality, we should now be able to accept a more abstract explanation of religious belief and of the Creator.

The clerics in any faith have an awesome responsibility, but have often failed in their duty to convey the truth of the message in the scriptures. This is often because they have not fully understood it themselves, although it is sometimes distorted deliberately. The great spiritual message that comes with each revelation has had to be contained within mere words, and sometimes words are not enough. For example, 'Omnipotent' (all-powerful) and 'Omniscient'(all-knowing) as a means of portraying God are two words that carry a lot of weight but still lack the depth of meaning that is required; words are not enough to encompass the reality of God as a Being possessing complete, unlimited, universal power and authority. Yet the Creator may still be 'known' through His creation. This is one reason why many find enlightenment through the natural world, as 'Abdu'l-Bahá describes:

> When, however, thou dost contemplate the innermost essence of all things, and the individuality of each, thou wilt behold the signs of thy Lord's mercy in every created thing, and see the spreading rays of His Names and Attributes throughout all the realm of being, with evidences which none will deny save the froward and the unaware. Then wilt thou observe that the universe is a scroll that discloseth His hidden secrets, which are preserved in the well-guarded Tablet. And not an atom of all the atoms in existence, not a creature from amongst the creatures but speaketh His praise and telleth of His attributes and names, revealeth the glory of His might and guideth to His oneness and His mercy: and none will gainsay this who hath ears to hear, eyes to see, and a mind that is sound.[19]

As each new age dawns, religions need to adapt, to be ready for the next stage of spiritual stock-taking that always occurs when a new Messenger appears. It is unfortunate that the man-made philosophies that have developed from the original teachings do not allow for this; they are merely analysing the established religion that they are familiar with and often not flexible enough to adapt to a new revelation. There are many references to a 'Return' in each faith system that indicates quite clearly it will be another Prophet or Messenger who will fulfil the promises and renew the teachings, but the clerics are unwilling to accept this possibility if it threatens their position, and they and do not generally indulge in consultation on such matters. It is more in their interest to foster belief in a way that supports their position and status. Unfortunately, this attitude, together with a vested interest in building power structures, encourages a tendency towards atheism without proof.

Faith versus no faith

When atheism dared to raise its head in the Age of Enlightenment at the end of the 18th century, it was claimed that reason was the only legitimate method of solving the meaning of life. This was later followed by the accusation that Creationists (not in this instance only those who follow the biblical account literally) were blind to the evidence of evolution. This accusation against established religion was not a valid criticism, for those of religious faith were mainly irritated that the new 'theory' of evolution appeared to rule out any possibility of a Creator. They were right to be wary of such a claim, because as we have seen and as 'Abdu'l-Bahá constantly reiterates, any Being that is defined as the Creator is completely and utterly beyond our ability to adequately describe or 'confine' by any sort of description.:

Every single manifestation of the myriad forms of creation is a reflection of the divine emanations, therefore the
divine emanations are infinite, unlimited and illimitable.
Gaze upward through immeasurable space to the majestic
order of the colossal suns. These luminous bodies are numberless. Behind our solar system there are unfathomable
stellar systems and above those stellar systems are the remote
aggregations of the milky way. Extend your vision beyond
the fixed stars and again you shall behold many spheres of
light. In brief, the creation of the Almighty is beyond the
grasp of the human intellect. When this objective creation is
unlimited and not subject to suspension, is not the subjective
creation of His Majesty the Almighty limitless? When the
reflection or physical creation is infinite, how is it possible to
circumscribe the reality which is the basis of divine creation?
The spiritual world is so much greater than the physical that
in comparison with it the physical world is non-existent.[20]

Generally (and one could even say, deliberately), atheists try to
confuse the issue by contrasting the laws of physics with the
religious concepts of an unknowable God. Believers in a spiritual Being that is involved in sending messengers to inspire
humanity can in no way conceptualize God in a way that
would be to the satisfaction of scientists or lay people. There
will always be mystery, but extremists or atheists will dismiss
religious teachings if they do not fit with their ideas, just as
politicians will fudge their agenda to appeal to the masses.
People should understand this and use their reasoning powers
to obtain full information before rushing to conclusions.
And it is not just the origin of life that is at present beyond
absolute certainty (still theoretical for scientists), but also the
claim that humans were latecomers in evolution and lucky to
have 'branched' from a line that favoured our development.
'Abdu'l-Bahá describes the Bahá'í position:

In the world of existence man has traversed successive degrees until he has attained the human kingdom. In each degree of his progression he has developed capacity for advancement to the next station and condition. While in the kingdom of the mineral he was attaining the capacity for promotion into the degree of the vegetable. In the kingdom of the vegetable he underwent preparation for the world of the animal and from thence he has come onward to the human degree or kingdom. Throughout this journey of progression he has ever and always been potentially man.[21]

Atheism as a belief system has created a divide and has itself become a pseudo-religious doctrine that uses an interpretation of evolution as its scripture. We should reiterate that a true understanding of the process of evolution does not and cannot undermine religious faith in a Creator. There is great difficulty in defining 'life' and its meaning, and science is still trying to explain fully how the inanimate can become animate. One possibility is that there is no such thing as inanimate matter – everything is always in motion: even that which appears to be still is composed of atoms and electrons in a state akin to vibration.

How can we explain this motion, this activity that exists at such deep levels of existence, except to say that there is always change? For the layman, animate means that which lives or moves, as opposed to inanimate, that which doesn't live or move. How, a person might ask, can 'non-living' become living?

These are ontological questions that can lead us around in circles, so perhaps we should be grateful to atheists for raising awareness of some of the limits of science as well as some of the illogical claims of religion. In some instances it may cause compliant believers to reexamine their belief and to understand that Darwin's theory of evolution can actually strengthen their faith through a much greater understanding of the beauty and complexity of creation. The 19th century with its proliferation of ideas has actually been a boon for people of faith, who had hitherto relied too heavily upon priestly explanations of the many mysteries within the writings of the various religions and now found that they could ask questions. It's just unfortunate that the questioning has led to so much acrimony.

So we may say that although committed atheists do not believe in a god or creator, they should not be castigated for this. It is their choice and it has led to all manner of arguments and disputes for and against the existence of God. On the other hand, they should not use their energy to try to deflect others from believing in God and wanting to live their lives in a state of ever-advancing spiritual understanding!

In between, there are the seekers and doubters who cannot come to a decision as to who is right. Yet the overwhelming majority of people do believe in a Creator or in a 'Something', although they may not be able to (or want to) spend their time trying to convince atheists that their faith helps them to find meaning in their lives. Atheists would also find it difficult to explain a mind/body experience and consciousness, whereas a religious person would identify this with a soul, and by extension with the existence of God. Of course, the religious person would have equal difficulty proving the existence of God to someone who is in denial, even though they have recourse to scripture and faith in what is revealed therein.

It is a quandary that affects both sides. Yet some of the attacks made by atheists are overtly political, in the sense that they are trying to exert power over those who disagree with them. Quite often the arguments descend into farce. For example, some atheists arrogantly dispose of the claim that prayer could possibly be of any benefit simply because they cannot see any physical proof of its efficacy, ignoring the positive effects of mental well-being that often arise from the simple act of prayer. Any supplication or meditative action obviously separates us from the animal kingdom, but tends to give atheists their greatest problem.

It is sheer arrogance for atheists to be the cause of dissension by demanding proof, without making a comparable effort to comprehend what has been revealed to humanity through the spiritual teachings of the Messengers. This unnecessary conflict confuses a lot of sincere people. Leaving aside those who believe that the universe was created just a few thousand years ago, it is now quite obvious that evolution has been long and gradual, and it is therefore quite logical, despite the protestations of some, to accept that there was a Cause behind this that we cannot understand.

Although we cannot really argue with the central theme of evolution and cannot actually prove to unbelievers that God or a Creator started it, we can *believe* and through that belief we can logically use the evidence from scripture that offers guidance on how we should conduct our lives and coexist in society, as revealed and explained by the divine Messengers and Prophets. Religious teachings help us to understand that there was, and is, a purpose to life. Atheists question that. We seem then to have become entrenched in two opposing camps, those who decry any form of belief in a Creator and those who cling, whether tenaciously or in doubt, to belief in a God Who created the universe.

O Children of the Divine and Invisible Essence! Ye shall be hindered from loving Me and souls shall be perturbed as they make mention of Me. For minds cannot grasp Me nor hearts contain Me.[22]

5

The Battle for Hearts and Minds

It is common practice for atheists to criticize the social rules and traditions instigated by religion. It is true also that many people are confused by religious teachings, having for too long accepted without too much investigation the interpretations of their religious leaders. It is therefore not surprising that many are all too eager to listen to the 'logical' interpretations of committed atheists. The New Atheists seem to have credible answers that offer to fill the mental void that the average person exhibits with regard to explanations of creation and evolution and the ethics or moral psychology that religious teachings have given them. In the absence of sensible explanations from most religious sources, atheistic attacks on religious scripture can also be seen as attacks on the faulty power structure that undermines the role of most religions today. It does not require great intellect to see that the man-made towers of pomp and power endemic in religious organization are sometimes built upon questionable foundations.

Perhaps the greatest enemy of religion is within its own ranks, because the harm that extremists of any religious persuasion may cause to their own followers is potentially enormous; it inevitably leads to schism. Such groups often rely heavily upon recruits from the poorly educated and/or fanatical elements who accept that their viewpoint is the 'only' way. The problems that lead to schism usually arise because the committed followers of some leader who has provided a new path to fulfilment will seldom respond to reason, so that any discussions are emotionally charged and it is extremely difficult to foster understanding between established sects. Some disagreements are so severe as to lead to murder and fanatical acts that are strongly condemned in the Holy Books and are not examples of true belief. Ideally, human beings should experience and exhibit feelings of joy, love, appreciation of beauty and unity when practising their faith.

Freedom of religion is actually supported by all the Prophets, for, as it says in the Qur'án, you cannot force people into belief (Sura 2.56), it has to come from within. However, illiteracy amongst believers is often a boon for power-seeking clerics of all faiths and explains why some extremist groups are particularly willing to destroy schools and educational opportunities. (Although, in the same way, politicians can influence a poorly educated population with rewards and promises and under some regimes may go so far as to rewrite their national history books.) Paying homage to or succumbing to intimidation from clergy who are keen to protect their power is no different from being coerced by political indoctrination. All of this contributes to the attraction of atheism.

Attacks on religious scripture

Into the agitation of the 19th century in religious and scientific circles (it had to happen sooner or later), Darwin, after years of travel and research, revealed a theory that overturned commonly held ideas about the origins and development of life on earth. Arguments immediately raged back and forth and forced many to reexamine their ideas of history and what had been promulgated through the scriptures. Long-established traditions of the Church were seriously questioned, and those in authority who had never before been challenged were now trying desperately to explain their age-old interpretations of scripture and creation. How life on earth began and how humanity itself had developed were now under question.

Intelligent people were no longer to be satisfied by the biblical teaching of the earth being created in seven days and the picturesque story of Adam and Eve. Many new 'learned societies' were formed as people sought ever more complex answers to the questions that were severely testing their received notions.

Even today, to ask a Creationist probing questions relating to scripture is to invite a barrage of insults, condemnation and the suggestion that it is the devil trying to deceive you. The devil was prominent in most religions and was often used as an explanation or analogy for evil or suffering; yet it was surely intended as a 'representation' of evil rather than a being of awesome independent power that could challenge God.

When Dawkins contrasts the stories of the Bible with scientific constructs as we know them today, he offers a sensible comparison and is quite right in saying that religious conviction can blind a person to the facts. But in the past (as in the present!), people when relating tales of their exploits relished exaggeration in order to impress their brethren and perhaps terrify their enemies. When attempting to explain the inexplicable they would often resort to analogy and imagery; this applies to a wide spectrum of prophetic tradition. Few could write or read, so many stories and legends were committed to memory. And it would be rare indeed to find an ancient document that has not been changed or distorted in some way in order to make a better story. Most modern people (with our experience of how the media privilege the 'story' over the facts) would accept that this is inevitable, and also that a certain amount of imagery would have been necessary to explain certain concepts to illiterate people.

This is why the constant assaults upon the chronicles that portray the history of religion are somewhat infantile attempts to undermine belief. Much would be lost if we were to ban myth and legend on the grounds that it is not literal fact. Bernard Shaw wrote:

All the sweetness of religion is conveyed to the world by the hands of storytellers and image-makers. Without their fictions the truths of religion would for the multitude be neither intelligible nor even apprehensible; and the prophets would prophesy and the teachers teach in vain.[1]

Shaw also famously remarked that we have not lost faith, merely transferred it to the medical profession.

Even though it is now self-evident that the earth is very ancient, certain religious sects have become stuck in a time-warp and stick doggedly with their interpretations of scripture. So the earlier myths and creation stories that fill the books of all the religions are constantly attacked from a 'scientific' view-point and it is perhaps, at the risk of being equally repetitive, better to offer up some of the more logical explanations at this point.

A striking example is the story of Noah's Ark; a picturesque story easily undermined by simple facts such as the sheer impossibility of travelling to collect all the species that needed to be saved from the Flood. This was perhaps conceded by the early story-tellers when they wrote that the animals were collected together and marched into the Ark. A literal interpre-tation of this does not consider the practicalities of finding the animals, arranging food storage and waste disposal and how quickly the earth could recover in order to support life; yet there are people who even today are trying to find the remains of an ark. An alternative and sensible explanation is that the Ark referred to faith itself, in other words, a refuge for believ-ers in the face of impending disaster. Noah was a Prophet, and when people were being attracted to idol worship and extreme lifestyles the Ark was the refuge that he offered against such dangers. The symbolism of the whole story (for the illiterate people of that age) helped them to understand and be pro-tected from the flood of superstition.

Meanwhile however, Dawkins persists to the point of

irritation and boredom with his attack on religious stories, such as the impossibility of a physical Ark. He makes no attempt to consider that there could possibly be other interpretations to this and other such traditions in the Bible, such as helping the blind to see (spiritually instead of physically). Even in his own field of expertise it may said of someone who cannot understand a certain concept that he is *blind to the reality* of the situation – a simple enough metaphor.

It should of course be obvious that many of the stories concerning the exploits of ancient peoples will have been greatly exaggerated in order to impress the believers or simply because they had no other way of explaining such wondrous events. True science was virtually non-existent and discoveries were few and far between. Adam, for example, was a Prophet whose task was to 'replenish' the earth spiritually ('Go forth and replenish the earth'[2]) and this has been true with all the Prophets that have appeared since.

And with regard to miracles – another target of Dawkins' wit – 'Abdu'l-Bahá explained that a literal interpretation was irrelevant to their true significance:

The outward miracles have no importance for the people of Reality. If a blind man receives sight, for example, he will finally again become sightless, for he will die and be deprived of all his senses and powers. Therefore, causing the blind man to see is comparatively of little importance, for this faculty of sight will at last disappear. If the body of a dead person be resuscitated, of what use is it since the body will die again? But it is important to give perception and eternal life – that is, the spiritual and divine life. For this physical life is not immortal, and its existence is equivalent to nonexistence. So it is that Christ said to one of His disciples: 'Let the dead bury their dead;' for 'That which is born of the flesh is flesh; and that which is born of the Spirit is spirit.'[1 Matt. 8:22; John 3:6.][3]

Now, at this point in our history, we believe we have many more answers that may help to understand the mystery of life than our predecessors could ever have imagined. Our knowledge base has grown and there is huge potential for advances in science and other disciplines and to further analyse historical influences and religious philosophy.

'The goal of all academic research is to find truth,' writes Udo Schaefer,

> yet religion is a subject that is only partially accessible to scientific analysis. The core of truth, the essential mystery of religion, is beyond the reach of science. There are no scientific criteria for a religion's claim to truth; it can be neither proven nor disproven scientifically. Scholars working in the field of religious studies can investigate and describe only the historical phenomenological and sociological aspects of their subject. The academic discipline of religious studies is by nature descriptive, narrative and comparative.[4]

How well were the original writings of the various religions understood, except perhaps by a favoured few? How many times have they been translated? What are the differences that cause such dissension between the different religions and the different sects of the same religion? Now, 2,000 years after the appearance of Christ, we are still getting new interpretations and re-evaluations in an effort to heal the rifts.

I would like to ask that instead of condemning the claims and traditions of theists, the New Atheists should perhaps consider, with all due fairness, the fact that such traditions may well have been misinterpreted according to the limitations of the age and the vested interest of clerics. After all, if anyone misinterprets evolution or Darwinism they are condemned as ignorant. New Atheists go to great lengths to drive home the point that the traditions of the major religions are open to ridicule, but do not mention Darwin's racial theories and ideas on eugenics. It is difficult to get committed believers to consider different interpretations, yet didn't Christ offer a fresh viewpoint and state that you cannot put new wine into old bottles? There has to be change.

Atheists also ask for 'evidence'. What sort of evidence would really convince them? Any evidence is scoffed at if it threatens their position. One striking example is prophecy, found in all the Holy Books of religion, and universally scorned by atheists. Yet prophecy has been one means by which people have structured their understanding of the future and hence their own present, and they continue to do so, both through religious prophecy and, for those who have rejected religion, frequent reliance on 'predictions' by astrologers or fortune-tellers. Yet accurate prophecies can be persuasive even though they cannot be shown to be conclusive, and unfortunately we can observe from history that people are only too eager to distort them to make them fit their own agenda. The question is, what is an accurate prophecy? What is reliable? For writer Gary Matthews, the position is clear:

> Prophecy is a prerogative God has reserved to Himself, for He clearly announces that 'there is none like me' in this respect. Prophetic foreknowledge, then, is a clear sign which no one – unaided by God – can replicate. God has chosen not to share this power with any false prophet, satanic deceiver or bogus messiah.[5]

Certain groups used this to point to the 19th century as being the 'time of the end', but then when events did not quite match their predictions they made 'adjustments' and reinterpreted. The most striking example was the results of the research carried out by the Millerites, followers of William Miller who in 1833 made announcements based upon his study of the Bible that the world would see the second advent of Christ in 1843. He gained a considerable following, but when events did not materialize as they had expected they subdivided into Bible study groups from which the Jehovah's Witness movement later emerged.

In attacking the soft targets that relate to the obscure traditions that were taught several thousand years ago, Dawkins is probably seeking popular approval. The employment of this method of undermining belief unfortunately detracts from serious discussion about why the great majority, whether they belong to a formal religious organization or not, believe in a power that caused and directs the universe and teaches us the essence of altruism by which we should organize our lives.

Ethics or moral psychology

When studying the various religions we should perhaps not attempt to compare their ethics, because the guidelines for each society/religion were revealed at certain periods in history to fit the exigencies of the age and it has therefore been a progressive process. While it is all too easy to ridicule those who believe that there is a Creator, it is not so easy to explain the source of ethical teachings that came via the religions and the subsequent rise in civilizations that can be linked with each one of them.

There are many ethical dilemmas for which there is guidance from scripture in all the religions, but atheists may well resort to their own interpretations. For instance, in this era of globalization the relationship between ethics and business has become important as never before. Questions are now being asked about whether business organizations and banks should be allowed to self-regulate, or should it be down to governments and economic gurus to place controls on them.

Some atheists also have a tendency to hijack humanism for their own ends, but in contrast to the missionary zeal of New Atheism, the general humanist approach is that if you believe in a god but do not try to force it upon others then they have no problem with it. Instead, they emphasize their belief that a person's capacities for self-realization through reason will eventually cause them to reject religion. However, when trying to rationalize something a scientist is expected to gather all the evidence and try to draw some comparisons between the knowledge and research that is available. It would be a poor scientist who refused to consider what proofs there would be that might challenge his observations. Ethics would be on rocky ground!

So from whence will come our ethical standards? Philosophers, scientists and atheists (even humanists) are all quite capable of misinterpreting or dismissing information if it does not support their arguments and beliefs. Where does the burden of proof lie?

Altruism

Dawkins' explanation of kindness, artistic prowess or altruism seems to be that it is an aberration and against evolution or natural selection, as the 'selfish gene' needs to survive 'at all costs'. This would appear to be quite a juvenile argument and an attempt to deny the possibility that such virtues might be encouraged, nurtured or inculcated by religious teachings that are responsible for the gradual progress of humanity. Let us extrapolate from the 'survival of the fittest' that some think would be the outcome of the 'selfish gene'. Couldn't that lead to the eugenics theories that were adopted by Hitler and his henchmen in their search for a super-race?

There is bound to be some disagreement over the claim that altruism is a product of genetic evolution. Surely altruism supported by the intrinsic moral guidance of religious teachings is a more positive cultural asset than man-made teachings or eugenics could provide? In fact, Dawkins later explained that in his book *The Selfish Gene* that the emphasis should be on '*Gene*':

The logic of Darwinism concludes that the unit in the hierarchy of life which survives and passes through the filter of natural selection will tend to be selfish. The units that survive in the world will be the ones that succeeded in surviving at the expense of their rivals at their own level in the hierarchy. That, precisely, is what selfish means in this context.[6]

However, there are other viewpoints.

According to Robert Trivers of Rutgers University in New Jersey, pure altruism is a mistake. He argues that natural selection favoured humans who were altruistic because in the small, close-knit groups in which our ancestors lived, altruists could expect reciprocity. However, in our globalised world where many of our interactions are with people we do not know and may never meet again, our altruistic tendencies are misguided: they are unlikely to be reciprocated and are therefore maladaptive.[7]

Yet altruism makes good evolutionary sense, even though it might appear that spending time and energy helping someone without any return may put you at a disadvantage. In a much-quoted passage by the novelist Ayn Rand on altruism (of which she disapproved):

The basic principle of altruism is that man has no right to exist for his own sake, that service to others is the only justification of his existence, and that self-sacrifice is his highest moral duty, virtue and value.

Although altruism is the essence of religion and the purpose of religion is the education of humanity, it is not correct to intimate, as Dawkins does in *The God Delusion* and other writings, that altruism could replace religion.

In our lives we find that without commitment to a cause

or unified action, success is limited, so we tend to join with others in seeking solutions. A possible negative aspect to this is the way some groups or ideologies can increase their influence over people's lives by persuasion, indoctrination or sheer power struggles. Whereas in the animal kingdom the 'herd' instinct is often necessary, and strong enough to bind groups together for survival, human beings have the advantage of free will with the emotional or 'spiritual' dimensions that go with it. This makes it necessary for altruistic leaders to appeal to the *inner* or idealistic part of our being that other life forms do not possess. In other words, the positive aspect is that there is an inner 'spiritual' conscience that can be influenced by example or teaching; the real you' that responds to selfless examples and can accept unity as a noble form of existence that is far beyond the herd instinct. It has marked us out from the beginning of evolution; man has always had a need to work with others, and a destiny, no matter what form or shape our evolutionary ancestors had.

Altruism of one sort or another is crucial for social cohesion. There are many social pressures that promote and encourage altruism, for example: reputation building, ideas of fairness, and guidance by family or authoritative religious leaders. There would certainly be instinctive as well as social pressures that are 'learned' from a superior. Even animals have their boundaries of what they tolerate from their off-spring and inferior members of the group, but one can argue that the rules of survival, which we could possibly view as altruistic, were usually adopted under the influence of teachings passed down by our ancestors as they began to create their social environment through mutually beneficial survival techniques. As early as the hunter–gatherer societies, the fear of being exiled or made an outcast was the ultimate weapon against anti-social behaviour; a worrying prospect that could only be countered by a group of exiles gathering sufficient support or possessing superior ideas or philosophies. Society is never static; otherwise it decays and faces collapse.

A common challenge to community life occurs when a particular community comes under the influence of a ruthless leader, or when new ideas are introduced and there is violent reaction against them so that a split occurs. The Soviet style of Marxism crushed the spirit of the proletariat and attempted to remove God from their lives, but it ultimately failed in this respect, for the existence of a society with only a man-made system of morals is akin to anarchy. It can produce only a system of rewards and punishments based upon materialistic values. The aftermath of war in devastated countries is witness to this; order has to be reestablished as quickly as possible.

The rule of law should be therefore based upon religious as well as secular ideas if it is to succeed, and each age requires 'a renewal of the blessed spring', in the words of 'Abdu'l-Bahá.[8] Such a renewal with its new ideas or philosophies often stems from the revolutionary teachings of a religious innovator.

In the ongoing debate between atheism and religion, whereby one side is committed to belief in God and the other denies that a God exists, it is only religion that can realistically claim to have enriched the lives of millions (leaving aside material possessions that are temporary). William Lane Craig, and American Christian philosopher and theologian, argues that without a 'theistic god' all our moral laws and the purpose of existence become illusory. In a way this is true, but the concept of free will as a gift from God puts a slightly different slant on it. With regard to evolution, one could postulate that the development of mind, intelligence and self-consciousness was vital to fully utilize the concepts and teachings that are necessary for the advance of civilization. Inherent within human evolution, free will is something that other species lack, and are therefore trapped in their instincts and desires. The gift of free will has also allowed us to express ourselves in a negative way, and there can be no greater test than this for humanity. We have the choice of accepting religious teachings or rejecting what we are taught, and we can deny God altogether. Of course, in a society that has a powerful religious structure there would be strong reaction to any suspected rejection of the teachings that are generally accepted and the image of God that is collectively worshipped. Religious traditions are a combination of history, custom and spiritual teachings that were intentionally formulated for the development of a moral society, and however primitive the concept, it was this that gave credence to the laws the society lived by.

Primitive man, who may be likened to a young child, would have conducted his life and actions with the over-riding motive of the immediate gratification of his needs and survival. A child is trained gradually in how to interact with others by the introduction of simple rules. Its free will is only slightly curtailed in this early training, simply because others must be protected from its actions as well as for its own personal safety. In time, the child's reasoning powers will help it, in the right environment, to work within the laws that make for a stable society. By using its free will and powers of reason the child should eventually come to understand that law and moral guidance are for the benefit of all. This is also the way that progressive revelation, from a chain of Prophets or Messengers, acts upon and guides humanity.

It is interesting that the 18th and 19th centuries produced so many philosophers. It was an age of enquiry and reason when great thinkers questioned the old ideas and produced volumes of writings, discoveries and inventions. 'The wisdom of every command shall be tested,' writes Bahá'u'lláh, referring to the appearance of the 'Most Great Beauty, foretold in the Books of the Messengers' during the 19th century,[9] while 'Abdu'l-Bahá spoke about the 'radiant century':

In the estimation of historians this radiant century is equivalent to one hundred centuries of the past. If comparison be made with the sum total of all former human achievements, it will be found that the discoveries, scientific advancement and material civilization of this present century have equalled, yea far exceeded the progress and outcome of one hundred former centuries. The production of books and compilations of literature alone bears witness that the output of the human mind in this century has been greater and more enlightening than all the past centuries together. It is evident therefore that this century is of paramount importance.[10]

In this age we have theoretically reached the age of maturity (in the spiritual sense, through divine revelation) and should find the solution within the revealed Word which exhorts us to help one another and to work together to eradicate poverty and suffering. We can no longer shut ourselves away from the problems of the world like the mystics of old, we must incorporate all the truths and experience into everyday life experience for everyone – helping those who cannot comprehend, or do not have the means, to enjoy the fruits of revelation for this age. This, it should be obvious, is the true objective of putting others first; altruism in all its glory, not just materially, but spiritually also. You may not have the ability to become a spiritual giant (how do we measure this anyway?) but could still help someone else to understand that the acquisition of knowledge is a good thing and giving up time to help others is even better. Voluntary contribution is not just about money – it is about support for others who may be in great need in any shape or form.

An example that comes to mind is a true story. A young blind man who could not read or write often listened to the words of a well-read person who would often come to their village and read to them from Bahá'í scriptures. Because he was unable to read, he memorized what he was taught and gradually understood the benefit of knowledge to humanity. As he became more confident he was able to travel and pass on this knowledge to help and guide others and became quite an accomplished speaker.

Knowledge shared
is knowledge gained,
however it is acquired
and whatever is attained.

The shape of things to come

Each and every major religion has at some time upset the applecart of established schools of thought by producing new fruit for consideration and discussion. Some of the fruit will seem bitter and will be rejected at first by the religious establishment. In *The God Delusion*, Dawkins seems not to have understood this, even though the same process occurs in science – this is the way progress is made. His statement that 'Jesus was not content to derive His ethics from the scriptures of His upbringing. He explicitly departed from them . . . when he deflated the dire warnings about breaking the Sabbath,'[11] exhibits a misunderstanding of the purpose of the Messengers. He does not, or perhaps cannot, differentiate between social and spiritual teachings. A new Messenger or Prophet renews the social laws for a new age whilst upholding the spirit of the original teachings: 'Not one jot or one tittle'[12] is subtracted from the spiritual guidance but social teachings have to be adjusted to suit changing circumstances. The fact that followers of the older faiths cling tenaciously to outmoded social teachings is one of the reasons that they do not investigate new teachings. It is a common failing.

Many historians are aware that the disintegration of a society usually takes place at the same time as a new one is being created, with the result that temporary chaos ensues. Many great changes throughout history have overlapped, insofar as renewal would be taking place alongside disintegration, a period of transition that could last for a long time. Many eminent historians have also noted that religion transformed society. How did it manage this? Mainly because, when new teachings appeared, the insiders or disciples led the way, with faith and fortitude, influencing society, introducing moral codes of conduct and injecting a spiritual dimension. They instigated progress for society; though not without opposition. Religious scripture is a combination of history, tradition, guidance and spiritual teachings for the development of a moral society. It is the people who resist change if they perceive it as a threat to their established way of life.

It is sensible to give consideration to the part evolution has played in steering humanity towards its destiny and to recognize that it has taken aeons to achieve this. From an historian's point of view evolution is beautiful and can only really be explained as an act of creation. But why deny that it had a 'goal' that culminated in humanity; producing conscious thinking beings that can make use of all the wonders that are around us? Man has always 'been'.

It may well seem, at this great distance in time, that the 'gods' of the early societies were supernatural creations – childlike projections of what people wanted a god to be. Such descriptions had their place, due to the limitations of the human mind to contain such a being. Yet we, as the created, still need to be nurtured. 'No matter to what religion a man belongs,' said 'Abdu'l-Bahá, 'even though he be an atheist or materialist, nevertheless, God nurtures him, bestows His kindness and sheds upon him His light.'[13]

Descartes is credited with the famous statement 'I think, therefore I am', and philosophers have used this for applying diverse meanings to human consciousness. It might be better to just say that we are *aware* **of** the world around us and are inquisitive about all aspects of life and the universe and this sets us apart from other species. We become more aware as we acquire more knowledge. To provide the answers that will change the world takes more effort than a philosophic discussion of man-made theories.

One philosopher who maintained that there is a direction

to history was Hegel (1770–1831). He exerted an immense influence during his lifetime that extended throughout Europe and is far beyond the scope of this book to discuss. Yet although he appeared to influence the age he lived in, he was in fact, like most philosophers, a product of that age. Through his ideas he tried to bring together a system of rules that would account for all the philosophical investigations that were the cause of intense discussion and dissent. Some of the apparent contradictions were those that concerned nature and freedom and the tendency to go beyond certain limits. While he had his supporters and opponents and influenced a large number of eminent thinkers, they nearly all avoided the alternative possibility that although science and philosophy are products of history, and the results of research are usually beneficial, it is the religious impulse that eventually appears to have the directive force that humanity needs for progress and fulfilment.

In 1862 Herbert Spencer attempted to reconcile science and religion, but upset both sides. It was perhaps a little too early. But Comte in 1845 had already concluded that the world could only be redeemed by a new religion (a fortuitous date from a Bahá'í perspective), but couldn't come up with anything apart from recycling old ideas when it was new teachings that were needed. In fact, at that very period in history (1844–65) the Báb and Bahá'u'lláh, who were in the process of revealing a new religion that actually highlighted the need to reconcile science and religion, were already promoting the new ideas.

Another point of view is that throughout history the abilities that have been shown through the natural process of evolution could be, and probably were, highlighted and exhibited by creative and inspired individuals who were ahead of their time and possessed attributes that were more than human. To avoid criticism and ridicule they had to drastically simplify what they were trying to instil in the minds of others, using symbolism and metaphor to explain while in expectation that it might well be resisted and condemned by those in authority, who would see it as a threat to their power. A number of destructive wars took place before the ideas were absorbed into human psyche. This description resembles the seers or prophets who were ahead of their time and who were at first recognized by very few enlightened individuals. Hence those who 'knew' would often take refuge in the wilderness or in a monastery. They had glimpsed the truth and understood eternity.

How does an atheist explain where all matter came from, apart from the Big Bang hypothesis, or come to terms with eternity? Even the Big Bang was a 'beginning' and this presupposes a Cause. Although atheists have a problem with there being a creator, they surely have more of a problem with the fact that life, in all its multifarious beauty and complexity and humanity with its conscious awareness of all that there is, has the hallmark of a Grand Design, as 'Abdu'l-Bahá explained:

> Is creation a manifestation or an emanation of God? There are two kinds of eternities. There is an eternity of essence, that which is without first cause, and an eternity of time, that which has no beginning. When you will understand these subjects all will become clear. Know of a certainty that every visible thing has a cause. For instance, this table is made by a carpenter; its originator is the carpenter. [14]

To begin to have some understanding of God we need communication channels, and such channels have been available throughout history through the Messengers or Prophets by means of revelation, in accordance with the limits of human comprehension in each age.

Surely, the most celebrated battle for hearts and minds today is between atheists and theists? Two entrenched viewpoints, each wielding weapons that they derive from their beliefs to convince their followers. Evolution was the strongest weapon in the armoury of the atheists, but when they were confronted by the challenge that the wonders of nature and the universe could only have come about through the power of creation by an all-powerful God, they failed to understand the true message of evolution. In view of the evidence, it is obviously saner to accept that evolution is a fact but that it nevertheless resulted through creation! Therefore there should be no conflict; but both sides need to re-evaluate their positions because it benefits no one when extremist views are promulgated and sensible discussion is moved to the sidelines. Science equals knowledge, religion equals reverence and insight, and they should be in harmony.

Great events obviously occurred in the 18th and 19th centuries, and considering world conditions at that time it was inevitable, though perhaps not desirable to some established institutions, that the world system had to undergo dramatic change and transition. A Bahá'í view of it all is given in *Who Is Writing the Future?*:

Particularly significant – because of its intimate relationship with the roots of human motivation – was the loosening of the grip of religious prejudice. Prefigured in the 'Parliament of Religions' that attracted intense interest as the nineteenth century was drawing to a close, the process of interfaith dialogue and collaboration reinforced the effects of secularism in undermining the once impregnable walls of clerical authority. In the face of the transformation in religious conceptions that the past hundred years witnessed, even the current outburst of fundamentalist reaction may come, in retrospect, to be seen as little more than desperate rear-guard actions against an inevitable dissolution of sectarian control. In the words of Bahá'u'lláh, 'There can be no doubt whatever that the peoples of the world, of whatever race or religion, derive their inspiration from one heavenly Source, and are the subjects of one God.'[15]

Although many no longer want to investigate new religious teachings, the appearance of the Bahá'í Faith at such an auspicious moment in history merits the closest attention. Since its inception it has been offering the peoples of the world a new understanding of the times they live in, not least through the pen of Shoghi Effendi, as in this statement to the Special UN Committee on Palestine as early as 1947 in the aftermath of the Second World War:

> ... this Faith is now increasingly demonstrating its right to be recognised, not as one more religious system superimposed on the conflicting creeds which for some many generations have divided mankind and darkened its fortunes, but rather as a restatement of the eternal verities underlying all the religions of the past, as a unifying force instilling into the adherents of these religions a new spiritual vigour, infusing them with a new hope and love for mankind, firing them with a new vision of fundamental unity of the religious doctrines, and unfolding to their eyes the glorious destiny that awaits the human race. [16]

6

The Purpose of Religion

Let us stop for a moment to reflect upon what has been achieved in this modern age that has given so many material benefits to such a large portion of humanity, as well as opportunities through modern technology to appreciate the vastness of space and the incredible complexity of the universe. So much has been achieved in the last two centuries that we should ask ourselves where the power to gain that knowledge can have come from. Everything seems to have come together in a veritable supernova of knowledge that has released spiritual and scientific tools for a new age. This is evolution of another sort; it has continued unabated into the 21st century and will continue to provide benefits into the future unless we fall into the abyss of selfish opportunism and suffer the loss of a spiritual dimension to our development.

Despite the efforts of so many practical and well-meaning enterprises, from the United Nations and its many agencies down to local charitable organizations too numerous to mention, a large proportion of the human race has so far missed out on the material growth and still struggles to exist, in abject poverty. Hope for a lasting improvement in conditions, with equal opportunities for participating in the material and spiritual wealth that this age will eventually provide, can come only through unity and a fair globalization.

We can only 'know' the reality and meaning behind it all through some channel that can reveal, for the generality of humankind, the true purpose of *being*. That channel would have to be universal and in a form of language that is commensurate with what all can understand.

We cannot rely on philosophers, who are themselves often influenced by the spirit of the past, to come up with solutions. Although they have grappled with the problem, the true reason for our existence has come to us through the teachings revealed by the Messengers, the Prophets, the Manifestations of God. But this potential can be realized only if humanity does not stay rooted in a time warp of teachings that have become outmoded, and instead reaches out to all of humankind as one family. The teachings of the major religions embrace the age-old 'Golden Rule' but are often too insular to put it into action.

The way forward is through acceptance that these advances in knowledge and opportunity are part of our spiritual development, and can manifest themselves in an infinite variety of personal experiences or through an understanding that humanity is one, and that divisions of race or religion are a hindrance to our spiritual evolution. 'Besides this,' said 'Abdu'l-Bahá,

> it is necessary that the signs of the perfection of the spirit should be apparent in this world, so that the world of creation may bring forth endless results, and this body may receive life and manifest the divine bounties. So, for example, the rays of the sun must shine upon the earth, and the solar heat develop the earthly beings; if the rays and heat of the sun did not shine upon the earth, the earth would be uninhabited, without meaning; and its development would be retarded. In the same way, if the perfections of the spirit did not appear in this world, this world would be unenlightened and absolutely brutal. By the appearance of the spirit in the physical form, this world is enlightened. As the spirit of man is the cause of the life of the body, so the world is in the condition of the body, and man is in the condition of the spirit. If there

were no man, the perfections of the spirit would not appear, and the light of the mind would not be resplendent in this world. This world would be like a body without a soul.

This world is also in the condition of a fruit tree, and man is like the fruit; without fruit the tree would be useless. [1]

Surely it cannot be denied that the real message is that humans (potentially) have an existence and sensitivity that transcends all other life forms and that they are spiritual in origin. It is the role of religion to explain the existence of God; in the words of Peter Medawar, 'science should not be expected to provide solutions to problems such as the purpose of life or the existence of God, for which it is unfitted'. [2]

Although atheists and humanists are sometimes eager to discuss the works of philosophers, they direct only ridicule toward those who follow a religion. Yet philosophers have only a limited influence upon the minds of men and their influence is often short-lived. In this era the speed of change has distorted the way of life of many people. Some cultures struggle to adapt, traditions are undermined and, as we have noted elsewhere, religious hardliners have turned to extremism to intimidate the generality of the people into keeping the faith; something that provides ample opportunities for atheists. However, the changes now affect every nation and all levels of society. The earlier civilizations used to fear the coming of the Barbarian hordes that threatened to destroy their way of life. In this age, according to Ian Angell, the barbarians are still with us but they have changed their image:

Make way for the barbarians (old and new), the opportunists awaiting their chance to hijack the future, and form a new order. The seeds of this new order are already here and they have already germinated. But are they friend or foe? They are the individuals, and transnational enterprises and companies that hold no herd loyalties. They are the press and media barons, the market manipulators, international business people, international terrorists, 'downsized' states, criminal conspirators, drug barons, neo colonialist non-governmental organizations, economic mercenaries, financial plutocrats, religious and political fundamentalists, amoral individualists: the new you and the new me? They are the power brokers, now cut free from the constraints of national boundaries by the new communication technologies.[3]

This is the new age, and the new reality that seems to accept a complete abandonment of ethics as a normal part of modern society is something that we have to face up to and come to terms with.

Religion is not just a binding force (*religare*) but a realization of a greater purpose and reality. Unfortunately it has often become a divisive instead of a unifying factor, due mainly to ignorance that gave ground to tribal forces and political influence and allowed some of the more extreme groups to use religion only as a label to rally the uneducated for support in their power struggles. Let us see what can be said about the necessity of an ethical way of life from a religious point of view that could turn the tide on modern barbarism and would surely have helped Darwin in his struggle over leaving God out of the equation. To start with, as Ulrich Gollmer points out,

No religion comes into being in an intellectual no man's land. Every religion addresses the needs of a particular people.[4]

'Abdu'l-Bahá, in a common-sense explanation of true evolution, writes that man has always been a distinct species.

But from the beginning of man's existence he is a distinct species. In the same way, the embryo of man in the womb of the mother was at first in a strange form; then this body passes from shape to shape, from state to state, from form to form, until it appears in utmost beauty and perfection. But even when in the womb of the mother and in this strange form, entirely different from his present form and figure, he is the embryo of the superior species, and not of the animal; his species and essence undergo no change. Now, admitting that the traces of organs which have disappeared actually exist, this is not a proof of the impermanence and the non-originality of the species. At the most it proves that the form, and fashion, and the organs of man have progressed. Man was always a distinct species, a man, not an animal. So, if the embryo of man in the womb of the mother passes from one form to another, so that the second form in no way resembles the first, is this a proof that the species has changed? that it was at first an animal, and that its organs progressed and developed until it became a man? No indeed! How puerile and unfounded is this idea and this thought! For the proof of the originality of the human species, and of the permanency of the nature of man, is clear and evident.[5]

In addition to this unique station, humanity has the bounty of being the recipient of ethical and spiritual teachings to assist in building civilizations that will be conducive to the progress of all. Each age has witnessed a 'renewal of the blessed spring' for the fulfilment of this destiny:

The prophets are sent to refresh the dead body of the world, to render the dumb, eloquent, to give peace to the troubled, to make illumined the indifferent and to set free from the material world all beings who are its captives. Leave a child to himself and he becomes ill-mannered and thoughtless. He must be shown the path, so that he may become acquainted with the world of the soul – the world of divine gifts.

Existence is like a tree, and man is the fruit. If the fruit be sweet and agreeable, all is well, but if it be bitter it were far better there were none. Every man who has known the celestial bestowals is verily a treasury; if he remain ignorant of them, his non-existence were better than his existence. The tree which does not bring forth fruit is fit only for the fire. Strive night and day to change men into fruitful trees, virgin forests into divine orchards and deserts into rose gardens of significance. Light these lamps, that the dark world may become illumined.[6]

It is true that religion has often been the cause of war and suffering, but this has been through human frailty and the result of perversions of the original teachings that had, in effect, been politicized. Because of this collapse in the integrity and purpose of organizations that were meant to safeguard and promulgate the morals and principles of religion, humanity has been assailed on all sides by examples of cruelty and suffering. The 19th and 20th centuries saw an astronomical rise in the death toll from war, pestilence, poverty and starvation.

'The face of the world', Bahá'u'lláh laments, 'hath altered. The way of God and the religion of God have ceased to be of any worth in the eyes of men.' 'The vitality of men's belief in God', He also has written, 'is dying out in every land . . . The corrosion of ungodliness is eating into the vitals of human society.' 'Religion', He affirms, 'is verily the chief instrument for the establishment of order in the world, and of tranquility amongst its peoples . . . The greater the decline of religion, the more grievous the waywardness of the ungodly. This cannot but lead in the end to chaos and confusion.' And again: 'Religion is a radiant light and an impregnable stronghold for the protection and welfare of the peoples of the world.' 'As the body of man', He, in another connection, has written, 'needeth a garment to clothe it, so the body of mankind must needs be adorned with the mantle of justice and wisdom. Its robe is the Revelation vouchsafed unto it by God.'[7]

The other-worldly view that has always given hope to religions was the belief that their Prophet would return in a blaze of glory, righting all the wrongs in an instant, even to a belief in 'raising the dead'; although it should be obvious that this term refers to the spiritually dead being transformed and made aware of spiritual truths. If a country or group has based its doctrines on emotionally distorted interpretations of religion, then that culture will find it daunting to even consider integrating with the rest of the world. Their own role models, the priests and leaders, are primed to extol a certain cultural image that has become the established 'truth' and they would find it extremely difficult to unite with others if it threatened to undermine their authority.

When a religious person claims to 'believe', this indicates that they have accepted the revelation that is the basis of their religion, not that they fully understand its core message. They thereby move from belief to faith, a loyalty that is not dependent upon full understanding. No Messenger or Prophet has ever condemned another major religion as being false, only that its followers have strayed and failed to understand what was taught.[8] Many centuries of distortion and misunderstanding have therefore been the cause of strife and deprivation. Certainly the priests and clerics of the major religions have a lot to answer for.

The atheist position, however, is more precarious from a truly scientific viewpoint. Despite the persistent declarations of atheists that God does not exist, how can the concept of a Creator be logically repudiated? There is not enough evidence for that. It becomes a prejudicial statement, denial through lack of evidence, and that is hardly scientific. The Creator, as an All-knowing God, has to be irreducibly complex by definition, and as such, this defeats all their arguments.

Evolution and ethics

Life evolves and religion also evolves. Atheists seem to be falling behind. We can understand that religious people can go astray and that sometimes science goes into an evolutionary dead-end, and both need to be renewed. Also, as has already been pointed out, the social teachings of religion become outmoded and the ethical teachings need to be strengthened, in keeping with the changing needs of an evolving humanity. Bahá'u'lláh reminds us that the purpose of divine revelation is the education of humanity:

> From the heaven of God's Will, and for the purpose of ennobling the world of being and of elevating the minds and souls of men, hath been sent down that which is the most effective instrument for the education of the whole human race.[9]

As we have seen earlier, historians have noted that the great changes throughout history have overlapped, with renewal taking place alongside disintegration. These periods of transition are essential, because human progress has always been a process of learning that has advanced at different speeds in diverse civilizations. There will usually be opposition, mainly because of the vested interests of those who have power and authority and who may oppose any change that would affect their status quo. When new teachings appear, the insiders or disciples lead the way, with faith and fortitude, slowly influencing and transforming society, introducing higher moral codes of conduct and a new spiritual dimension. Thus we observe the process of disintegration and integration taking place within the same period of time.

These dynamic periods of growth could not have happened without a religious dimension that could inject a spiritual energy into the affairs of humankind. As a modern analogy, we might borrow from the world of physics and suggest that *fission* could represent the release of the spiritual energy from the Word of God that would induce unity in the human world. This would later be followed by *fusion*, indicating the powerful results that will ultimately come from that unity; and this is surely the destiny for this age.

We know that we cannot view the sun with the naked eye; if we are to study its processes and make sense of it all we need special instruments. Likewise, when we wish to peer down into the quantum world we again need special instruments. We require, in the words of 'Abdu'l-Bahá, 'the tools of perception and knowledge' if we are to reach out to God, and these come with the appearance of the Prophets, the teachings that they bring, and a profound faith. Atheist writings are utterly devoid of such benefits.

With regard to another belief system, pantheism, and its rejection of a 'personal' God, the arguments can be very confusing. Because of this, some are minded to label a pantheist as an atheist and both sides are liable to go into dialectical discussions that lead nowhere. Perhaps pantheism could be seen as more reverent and the reason why Dawkins is quoted as saying that 'pantheism is sexed-up atheism'.

We all need to engage in the ideas and discourse of the society we live in; it is part of the learning process that permeates modern thought and sometimes leads to the use of dialectics in trying to keep pace with new terminology and the advances in science. 'Put all your beliefs into harmony with science,' said 'Abdu'l-Bahá,

> there can be no opposition, for truth is one. When religion, shorn of its superstitions, traditions, and unintelligent dogmas, shows its conformity with science, then will there be a great unifying, cleansing force in the world which will sweep before it all wars, disagreements, discords and struggles – and then will mankind be united in the power of the Love of God.[10]

Supporters of the theory of evolution are still seeking to bring the threads together to make a fitting garment for scientific study, and some religious observers are seeking, within the confines of their beliefs, to find common ground and bring the ultimate truth into the realm of human thought. This struggle highlights the fact that science and politics have replaced religion in many parts of the world and are controlling the minds of the population in much the same way as many religious leaders have done throughout history.

Meanwhile, atheists will continue to attack extremism in religion, and why not? When a so-called Jihadist kills and maims in the name of religion, it is rightly condemned, for they are not truly representative of the faith that they proclaim. When schools are burned, this cannot be put down to religious belief; it is fear of what the results of education might bring. This is a sad development, given that at one time Islam led the world in education and science that led to some of the first universities being created.

In this age the cosmologists have been taking centre stage, as new and more powerful telescopes enhance their knowledge of the universe and not only instil a sense of wonder and humility but surely indicate beyond reasonable doubt that there is a creative force behind it. Gravity seems to be fine-tuned and constant, and all life forms need gravity to help them function. Some physicists have also been quoted as saying that electrons don't *exist,* but for the layman this is probably too difficult to grasp. Physicists are grappling with a concept of *existence* relating to an entity that they know through its behaviour and effects, but cannot truly conceptualize for others. They also feel the need to have faith in the results of their research before they can fully understand. Isn't this also the way a religious person feels about God?

Such profound discussions are probably beyond the scope of this book, yet these examples may be useful to illustrate that there are many mysteries that both the atheist and the religiously-minded scientist have to resolve if they are to present their claims as logical conclusions that could satisfy all. There is, then, some common ground and this is further proof that harmony between religion and science could prove fruitful for both. Science has achieved so much since the 19th century, both constructive and destructive, but science must serve humanity, not the other way around

In his book *The God Delusion*, Dawkins probably made an error of judgement in going outside his scientific explorations of evolution when he ranted so much against religion. The study of evolution concerning humankind can be important if it doesn't keep comparing human with animal behaviour. Science has its true domain in the scientific method, but it should not stray into fields which it cannot ultimately fathom. In reviewing Dawkins' book, Stephen Phelps writes,

> Central to Dr. Dawkins' project of dismantling the foundations of religious belief is an attack on what he calls 'the God hypothesis' – the idea 'that the reality we inhabit also contains a supernatural agent who designed the universe and – at least in many versions of the hypothesis – maintains it and even intervenes in it with miracles, which are temporary violations of his own otherwise grandly immutable laws'.
>
> The arguments in the first half of *The God Delusion* flow from this assertion, beginning with a solid, if at times dismissive, rebuttal of the traditional proofs for God's existence and culminating in an exposition on how evolution explains how life might arise through a gradual and cumulative process without the need to invoke an intelligent designer. Indeed, Dawkins argues that a designer of the kind defined by his 'God hypothesis' must be even more improbable than its handiwork.
>
> When set against traditional religious understandings of God, Dr. Dawkins' arguments are quite powerful. But against the Bahá'í understanding of God and nature, the

contradictions that he identifies between science and religion simply dissolve.[11]

We also have to recognize that some of religious history is fiction, based upon a devout wish to believe, in the absence of absolute proof. Unfortunately the fiction, allied with tradition, then takes on its own powerful stimulus and aura of sacredness. But there is hope, as the supreme governing body of the Bahá'í Faith expressed in a message to the religious leaders of the world in 2002:

> Because it is concerned with the ennobling of character and the harmonizing of relationships, religion has served throughout history as the ultimate authority in giving meaning to life. In every age, it has cultivated the good, reproved the wrong and held up, to the gaze of all those willing to see, a vision of potentialities as yet unrealized. From its counsels the rational soul has derived encouragement in overcoming limits imposed by the world and in fulfilling itself. As the name implies, religion has simultaneously been the chief force binding diverse peoples together in ever larger and more complex societies through which the individual capacities thus released can find expression. The great advantage of the present age is the perspective that makes it possible for the entire human race to see this civilizing process as a single phenomenon, the ever-recurring encounters of our world with the world of God. [12]

So is it possible that the impending globalization of our planet is going to achieve the final goal of unity in diversity; providing equal opportunities for all? Could this be achieved without a powerful unifying factor such as religion? Every nation will need to solve this problem, and every nation would be required to make sacrifices in pursuit of this goal: at present, they prefer to make sacrifices only in the pursuit of profit.

It is apparent that transition in human society is a process of change, whether social or religious. Every revelation of a divine religion has taken this into account, and every Prophet spoke in the language of the age. This era of globalization is no different. There is a 'turning point', as Capra describes in his book of that title:

> In the emerging world of living systems mind is not a thing, but a process. It is cognition, the process of knowing, and it is identified with the process of life itself.[13]

In Communist ideology religion was anathema, the so-called 'opium of the people' (Karl Marx). The salvation preached by the different religions was therefore hijacked by socialism. It was to be all that man had dreamed of since the French Revolution – liberty, equality and fraternity, not through religious means but through the efforts and brotherhood of the workers – atheism in all its promised glory that failed to deliver. Likewise, science and materialism are but temporary palliatives in a fast-changing world; they are certainly not the cure, often providing a quick fix but not a lasting remedy. Yet if we seek a spiritual answer from the contending faiths we may be confused by a plethora of 'solutions'. Schaefer describes the dilemma:

> Notions of value are of an axiomatic nature; no logical proof of their correctness can be supplied. Therefore neither reason nor science are adequate tools for providing standards of value or defining aims. Science is not competent to deal with moral issues. It cannot derive a watertight system of ethics. Ethical norms cannot be simulated in a computer. How a human being should behave in order to live a fulfilled and self-determined life cannot be defined in scientific terms.[14]

How we behave, and the standards expected in society, are

usually set against what has been introduced by religious teachings that are thus empowered to revitalize society. In the words of Alexander Solzhenitsyn in the Templeton Address of 1983:

> All attempts to find a way out of the plight of today's world are fruitless without a repentant return of our consciousness to the Creator of all . . . In the life of our entire planet, the Divine Spirit moves with no less force: this we must grasp in our dark and terrible hour.

Having put forward spirituality as a defining issue in the life of humanity, we have to attempt to explain spirituality in a way that might be acceptable to atheists if they are open-minded enough to consider it. It is the backlash from disbelief in religious ideals that causes a complete denial of God or a move into extremism. Meanwhile, the breakdown of morality is rampant in every civilized nation of the world. Shoghi Effendi warned the Bahá'ís:

> People are so markedly lacking in spirituality these days that the Bahá'ís should consciously guard themselves against being caught in what one might call the undertow of materialism and atheism, sweeping the world these days. Scepticism, cynicism, disbelief, immorality and hard-heartedness are rife, and as friends are those who stand for the antithesis of all these things they should beware lest the atmosphere of the present world affects them without their being conscious of it.[15]

But atheists cannot really come up with convincing arguments to undermine sincerely held beliefs and so they resort to lashing out at the myths and traditions, choosing conflict over compromise. The only 'new' thing about 'New Atheism' is that it is now easier to proclaim that they do not believe, whereas in the past it was a dangerous thing to advertise – and still is in some parts of the world where tolerance and free thinking are in short supply. From the atheist viewpoint, the weaknesses of religion lie in its claims to exclusivity and its inflexible doctrines; however, the atheist movement itself is in total disarray, with many independent spokespersons having no really outstanding characteristics apart perhaps from some acquired knowledge in the arena of philosophy.

Meanwhile, the 'other-worldly' claims of religious groups are many, in addition to which 'rewards' are offered to a believer, although these have to be taken on trust and supported by faith in the teachings of a Prophet/Founder. Unfortunately, some religious extremists would kill to defend their views because they believe that they will be rewarded in an afterlife for carrying out such acts. This, quite naturally, causes atheists (and many theists for that matter) to ask what right a religious organization can possibly claim that allows them to take life in the name of their religion. It is so obviously a distortion of scripture that unfortunately plays into the hands of atheists.

Another weakness of some religious movements is that they will not tolerate free and open discussion about their core beliefs. In recent years, for example, there have been perceived problems about religious attitudes to homosexuality. If homosexuality is forbidden in the teachings of a religion, then there is a duty to explain that this is not the same as persecution, but a religious law that should be obeyed if at all possible. Most tolerant religious movements would say that a homosexual would be welcome to join them but that homosexual acts are not condoned. Regrettably, conservative thought and political opportunism from both sides can poison the waters of informed debate.

It is also quite common to find people who believe profoundly in the importance of upholding common moral law and yet they cannot believe that the moral laws have been influenced or initiated by religion. This line of thought is a form of philosophy, sometimes called humanism, that asserts that human dignity and man's capacity for fulfilment through reason and scientific method is sufficient. So far, there is little evidence of this – it is a kind of wishful thinking that would justify the idea that religion is unnecessary.

And what of death? Sincere belief in an afterlife, as the next stage in our spiritual journey, is derived from religion and is considered to be a specific stage in our journey where we will be called to account for our actions. To the atheist, death is the end, while to the theist it can be the beginning, something that they either fear or welcome. In Shakespeare's words:

> But that the dread of something after death,
> The undiscover'd country from whose bourn
> No traveller returns, puzzles the will
> And makes us rather bear those ills we have
> Than fly to others that we know not of? [16]

The constant assaults by atheists and humanists are actually causing many religious people to re-examine the history and teachings of their faith, and sometimes this is not such a bad thing, especially as non-believers are constantly revising their positions also. This can lead to informed debate; in either camp, it is important to discover the truth, as this is part of our spiritual evolution and free will. George Townshend writes:

> Spiritual evolution does not move forward through any coercion of the wills of men. God requires that men of their own volition shall co-operate with Him. He does not substitute His will for their wills, nor does He, so to speak, drive their development onward by any output of main force. He educates and trains them little by little and measures His requirements to their growing strength of mind and heart. Those Supreme Prophets, therefore, who are His Agents and the Masters of Evolution, are limited by the capacity of the people. They cannot put a bushel of truth into a pint measure.

They cannot teach more than their hearers can learn.[17]

To the annoyance of atheists, theists insist that the universe needs an explanation beyond what science can ever provide. Conversely, in *Arguing for Atheism* Robin Le Poidevin writes:

> A world in which there can be causal explanation is not a chaotic world; it is a world tightly constrained by the laws of nature. Causal generalisations are simply reflections of these laws: that is, they are true because of the existence of fundamental laws. *Causal explanation, then, takes place against a background of laws.*[18]

Another viewpoint comes from the Bahá'í teachings:

> Now as to the infinite Power that knoweth no limitations; limitation itself proveth the existence of the unlimited, for the limited is known through the unlimited, just as weakness itself proveth the existence of power, ignorance the existence of knowledge, poverty the existence of wealth. Without wealth there would be no poverty, without knowledge no ignorance, without light no darkness. Darkness itself is a proof of the existence of light for darkness is the absence of light.[19]

If religion is the guiding moral force for humanity, then it is extremely important to examine the ideas and teachings that have renewed religion throughout history and provided the impetus for the spiritual renewal of civilization. The teachings of Baha'u'llah were and are revolutionary; way ahead of what the generality of humankind was ready for in the mid-19th century:

- The oneness of humanity

- The equality of women and men

- The elimination of prejudices

- The elimination of extremes of wealth and poverty

- The independent investigation of truth

- Universal education

- Religious tolerance

- The harmony of science and religion

- A world commonwealth of nations

- A universal auxiliary language

Despite widespread recognition of these standards in the 21st century, humanity is still struggling with how to implement them with justice and understanding. We still do not know how they will be interpreted and utilized in the future. For example, consider one of the important principles established in the teachings of Bahá'u'lláh: the equality of men and women. Although much has been achieved in the past hundred years, gender equality has not been a high priority in the older religions; this was probably intended to protect women. The task now is to educate the masses into changing their attitudes to the role that women can play in society. It is quite obvious that the emancipation of women in many parts of the world has released their talents and raised awareness of their aptitudes. This has not come without cost, especially in the reactions from male supremacists, but there is now worldwide recognition of the valuable contributions that women have been able to make to modern society. Capra comments of this revolutionary change:

The power of patriarchy has been extremely difficult to

understand because it is all-pervasive. It has influenced our most basic ideas about human nature and about our relation to the universe – 'man's' nature and 'his' relation to the universe, in patriarchal language. It is the one system which, until recently, had never in recorded history been openly challenged, and whose doctrines were so universally accepted that they seemed to be laws of nature; indeed, they were usually presented as such. Today, however, the disintegration of patriarchy is in sight. The feminist movement is one of the strongest cultural currents of our time and will have a profound effect on our further evolution.[20]

Seventy years earlier, 'Abdu'l-Bahá had said in London:

This is the age of woman. She should receive the same education as her brother and enjoy the same privilege; for all souls are equal before God. Sex, in its relation to the exigencies of the physical plane, has no connection with the Spirit. In this age of spiritual awakening, the world has entered upon the path of progress into the arena of development, where the power of the spirit surpasses that of the body. Soon the spirit will have dominion over the world of humanity.[21]

To see religion as continuous and progressive throws new light upon the importance of faith as something that can bring unity and allow religionists to reject the errors that have led to confusion, division and power-seeking. When we consider religious teachings as progressive we can then understand that there is really only one religion, that has been expressed throughout history in the religions we know by their different names. The scriptures have always had to be explained to the people because, as Moses Maimonides (12th century CE) stated, 'the purpose behind the laws of the Torah was evident in very few of them'.

To deny or accept, or at least to investigate with an open

mind, is an aspect of our free will. This does not mean destroying opposing views, as is common in political debate, but studying and weighing up the evidence. If scientists ignore or fail to investigate evidence at their disposal they are rightly castigated. When a believer points to what they feel is significant evidence for their beliefs, they should be respected and their evidence considered, rather than dismissed out of hand. Some atheists attempt to put the burden upon theists to 'prove' that there is a God, in spite of the fact that, as mentioned earlier, it is impossible for finite beings to describe the infinite. The real challenge is for the atheists to prove beyond doubt that there is no God. 'Abdu'l-Bahá responded to many questions on this subject; for example:

> The materialists state that inasmuch as it is proved by science that the life of phenomena depends upon composition and its destruction upon disintegration, they question the necessity of a creator, the self-subsistent Lord. 'For,' argue the materialists, 'we see with our own eyes that these infinite beings go through myriads of forms of composition and in every combination they bring about certain distinctive characteristics, so we are independent of any divine maker.'
>
> Those informed with divine philosophy answer that there are three theories of composition: first, accidental composition; second, involuntary composition; third, voluntary composition.
>
> If we declare that construction is accidental, this is logically a false theory, because then we have to believe in an effect without a cause; our reason refuses to think of an effect without a primal cause.
>
> The second, involuntary composition, means that each element has within it an innate function of this power of composition – certain elements have flowed toward each other, their union being an inherent necessity of their being. But as long as we reason that it is the inherent necessity of

those elements to enter into composition there should not be any necessity for decomposition; and inasmuch as we observe that there is a process of decomposition, we conclude that the constituent elements of life enter neither involuntarily nor accidentally, but voluntarily into composition – and this means that the infinite forms of organisms are composed through the superior will, the eternal will, the will of the living and self-subsistent Lord.

This is a rational proof that the will of the Creator is effected through the process of composition . . .[22]

The writings of Bahá'u'lláh and 'Abdu'l-Bahá point to the transcendence of this Supreme Being:

All superior kingdoms are incomprehensible to the inferior; how therefore could it be possible that the creature, man, should understand the almighty Creator of all?[23]

Were the Eternal Essence to manifest all that is latent within Him, were He to shine in the plenitude of His glory, none would be found to question His power or repudiate His truth. Nay, all created things would be so dazzled and thunderstruck by the evidences of His light as to be reduced to utter nothingness. How, then, can the godly be differentiated under such circumstances from the froward?[24]

While many have put their trust in science to explain the mystery of the universe and our origins, others leave it to religion. It is perhaps unfortunate that the numbers of people committed to religion has been dropping in recent years, but it is often organized religion itself that is putting people off. Each and every Prophet came into the world when true belief was at a low ebb, with the task of revitalizing belief in God. 'Abdu'l-Bahá reminded his listeners:

Recollect that Christ, solitary and alone, without a helper or protector, without armies and legions, and under the greatest oppression, uplifted the standard of God before all the people of the world, and withstood them, and finally conquered all, although outwardly He was crucified. Now this is a veritable miracle which can never be denied. There is no need of any other proof of the truth of Christ.[25]

There has been a systemic failure by the leaders of the established religions to put their message across, together with a lack of curiosity and/or understanding by those who have rejected structured religion in favour of 'freedom'. This has led to a proliferation of cults with some bizarre results that are obviously beyond the scope of this book. But even when a dubious sect distorts scripture for the purpose of exerting control, the things that are banned often appear quite alluring. Ron Hubbard, founder of Scientology, famously claimed that to make money one only needed to invent a religion. Of course, such statements only encourage those who constantly seek to ridicule religious belief. 'It is evident therefore', said 'Abdu'l-Bahá,

that counterfeit and spurious religious teaching, antiquated forms of belief and ancestral imitations which are at variance with the foundations of divine reality must also pass away and be re-formed. They must be abandoned and new conditions be recognized. The morals of humanity must undergo change. New remedies and solutions for human problems must be adopted. Human intellects themselves must change and be subject to the universal reformation. Just as the thoughts and hypotheses of past ages are fruitless today, likewise dogmas and codes of human invention are obsolete and barren of product in religion. Nay, it is true that they are the cause of enmity and conducive to strife in the world of humanity; war and bloodshed proceed from them and the oneness of mankind finds no recognition in their observance. Therefore it is our duty in this radiant century to investigate the essentials of divine religion, seek the realities underlying the oneness of the world of humanity and discover the source of fellowship and agreement which will unite mankind in the heavenly bond of love. This unity is the radiance of eternity, the divine spirituality, the effulgence of God and the bounty of the Kingdom. We must investigate the divine source of these heavenly bestowals and adhere unto them steadfastly. For if we remain fettered and restricted by human inventions and dogmas, day by day the world of mankind will be degraded, day by day warfare and strife will increase and satanic forces converge toward the destruction of the human race.[26]

The teachings of a true religion are presented according to the capacity and understanding of the age and their purpose is to promote 'an ever-advancing civilization'. Modern extremes lead to a loss of community values and ignorance of the inner spirituality that should inspire and unite us and give us a sense of purpose. The corruption in modern society, whether it is by big business in the pursuit of profit, or by governments that abuse their responsibility to care for the people and instead divert money to profitable weapons, is symptomatic of the extreme loss of values and ethics that stem from the impairment of virtue and moral principles. Despite this, it would seem that the more religious belief is attacked – and it is usually to ridicule the ideas and teachings – the stronger is the determination to believe or understand. As Phillip Allott writes:

Religion is as natural to a human being as thinking. To will and to act is, for a human being, to will and to act through consciousness in accordance with value under the impulse of desire and within the constraint of obligation. It is natural, therefore, that reflexive and reflective consciousness will seek to find a theory to reconcile, within a single structure of significance, all willing and acting, all values, all desire and obligation, all the impulse of life and all of the necessity of the universe. Such is the function of religion.[27]

Chance, rather than certainty, seems to dominate the ideas of the irreligious but there are some scientists who have insights that stem from their material investigations and lead them to a spiritual understanding of life. Fritjof Capra describes one of his experiences:

I was sitting by the ocean one late summer afternoon, watching the waves rolling in and feeling the rhythm of my breathing, when I suddenly became aware of my whole environment as being engaged in a gigantic cosmic dance. Being a physicist, I knew that the sand, rocks, water and air around me were made of vibrating molecules and atoms, and that these consisted of particles which interacted with one another by creating and destroying other particles. I knew also that the Earth's atmosphere was continually bombarded by showers of 'cosmic rays', particles of high energy under-going multiple collisions as they penetrated the air. All this was familiar to me from my research in high-energy physics, but until that moment I had only experienced it through graphs, diagrams and mathematical theories. As I sat on that beach my former experiences came to life. I 'saw' cascades of energy coming down from outer space, in which particles were created and destroyed in rhythmic pulses; I 'saw' the atoms of the elements and those of my body participating in this cosmic dance of energy; I felt its rhythm and I 'heard' its sound, and at that moment I knew that this was the Dance of Shiva, the Lord of Dancers worshipped by the Hindus.[28]

For science and religion it has been a long journey. The investigative potential of science has enriched our material lives and the history of religion has illuminated the gems of divine guidance that will protect us, if we pay heed, from the excesses of human weakness. Eventually the meeting of minds that will result from a harmony of religion and science in a passionate embrace of service and belief will enhance every aspect of our existence. The agents of change that have been set in motion by the belief in a Supreme Being cannot be reversed.

At the risk of abuse from atheists worldwide, I submit the suggestion that now, despite the apparent set-backs and doubts, we will see that globalization, world unity and peace will ultimately come about through the influence of religion rather than politics, technology or anything else (although these all have a part to play), for the Golden Rule still influences much of human thought and action. If all the religions humbly sit down together and consult on the main principles enshrined in their scriptures they will come to an understanding that they have the solution within their grasp. The modern interfaith movements are a sign that it is possible to subsume some of their treasured precepts for the greater good.

So how do we conclude a discourse upon atheism and belief? Surely both sides are so entrenched that that their positions are immovable? I personally think that the situation has been transformed in recent years and while some theists are becoming more appreciative of the difficulties of atheists to come to terms with the concepts of God and established religious traditions, many more atheists are beginning to see that it is self-defeating to keep attacking the many belief systems and to attempt to provide alternative explanations for the purpose of life and the universe. Day by day we are confronted with newly discovered facts about the world we live in, both in the cosmos and in the quantum world, and the questions become more urgent. Because of this, I submit that the meaning of life and the much needed *renewal of civilization* is unlikely to come from atheistic ideas. In the Bahá'í view,

The endowments which distinguish the human race from all other forms of life are summed up in what is known as the human spirit; the mind is its essential quality. These endowments have enabled humanity to build civilizations and to prosper materially. But such accomplishments alone have never satisfied the human spirit, whose mysterious nature inclines it towards transcendence, a reaching towards an invisible realm, towards the ultimate reality, that unknowable essence called God. The religions brought to mankind by a succession of spiritual luminaries have been the primary link between humanity and that ultimate reality, and have galvanized and refined mankind's capacity to achieve spiritual success together with social progress.[29]

Bibliography

'Abdu'l-Bahá. *'Abdu'l-Bahá in London* (1912, 1921). London: Bahá'í Publishing Trust, 1982.

— *Abdul Baha on Divine Philosophy.* Comp. I. F. Chamberlain. Boston: The Tudor Press, 1918.

— *Paris Talks: Addresses given by 'Abdu'l-Bahá in 1911* (1912). London: Bahá'í Publishing Trust, 12th ed.1995.

— *The Promulgation of Universal Peace: Talks Delivered by 'Abdu'l-Baha During His Visit to the United States and Canada in 1912* (1922, 1925). Comp. H. MacNutt. Wilmette, IL: Bahá'í Publishing Trust, 2nd ed. 1982.

— *Selections from the Writings of 'Abdu'l-Bahá.* Comp. Research Department of the Universal House of Justice. Haifa: Bahá'í World Centre, 1978.

— *Some Answered Questions* (1908). Comp. L. Clifford Barney. Wilmette, IL: Bahá'í Publishing Trust, 3rd ed. 1981.

— 'Tablet to Dr. Auguste Henri Forel', in *The Bahá'í World 1968– 1973*, vol. XV (Haifa: Bahá'í World , pp. 37–43.

Allott, Philip. *Eunomia: New Order for a New World.* Oxford: Oxford University Press, 1991, 2001.

Angell, Ian. *The New Barbarian Manifesto.* London: Kogan Page, 2000.

Bahá'í International Community. *A Bahá'í Declaration of Human Obligations and Rights*, presented to the first session of the United Nations Commission on Human Rights, February 1947.

One Common Faith. Haifa: Bahá'í World Centre, 2005.

Who is Writing the Future? Haifa: Bahá'í World Centre, 1999.

Bahá'í Prayers: A Selection of Prayers Revealed by Bahá'u'lláh, The Báb, and 'Abdu'l-Bahá. Wilmette, IL: Bahá'í Publishing Trust, rev. ed. 1991.

Bahá'í World Faith: Selected Writings of Bahá'u'lláh and 'Abdu'l-Bahá. Wilmette, IL: Bahá'í Publishing Trust, rev. ed. 1956.

Bahá'u'lláh. *Epistle to the Son of the Wolf.* Trans. Shoghi Effendi. Wilmette, IL: Bahá'í Publishing Trust, rev. ed. 1976.

— *Gleanings from the Writings of Bahá'u'lláh.* Trans. Shoghi Effendi. Wilmette, IL: Bahá'í Publishing Trust, 2nd ed. 1976.

— *The Hidden Words of Bahá'u'lláh.* Trans. Shoghi Effendi. Wilmette, IL: Bahá'í Publishing Trust, 1970; New Delhi: Bahá'í Publishing Trust, 1987.

— *Kitáb-i-Íqán: The Book of Certitude.* Trans. Shoghi Effendi. Wilmette, IL: Bahá'í Publishing Trust, 2nd ed. 1950, 1981.

— *Tablets of Bahá'u'lláh Revealed after the Kitáb-i-Aqdas.* Comp. Research Department of the Universal House of Justice. Haifa: Bahá'í World Centre, 1978.

Bible. *Holy Bible.* King James version. London: Eyre and Spottiswoode, various dates.

Capra, Fritjof. *The Tao of Physics.* Berkeley, CA: Shambala, 1975.

— *The Turning Point: Science, Society, and the Rising Culture.* New York, Simon and Schuster, 1982.

Darwin, Charles. *On the Origin of Species.* London: John Murray, 1859.

Dawkins, Richard. *The God Delusion.* London: Bantam, 2006.

— *The Selfish Gene.* Oxford: Oxford University Press, 2006.

Dingle, Herbert. *The Scientific Adventure: Essays.* New York: Philosophical Library, 1953.

Esslemont, J. E. *Bahá'u'lláh and the New Era.* Wilmette IL: Bahá'í Publishing Trust, 1980.

Fukuyama, F. *The End of History and the Last Man.* New York: Free Press, 1992.

— *Trust: The Social Virtues and the Creation of Prosperity*. New York: Free Press, 1995.

Gail, Marzieh. *Dawn Over Mount Hira and other essays*. Oxford: George Ronald, 1976.

Gandhi, M. K. *Young India: 1919-1931*. 13 vols. Ahmedabad: Navajivan, 1981.

Gefter, Amanda. 'Q & A': 2008 Templeton Prize winner', in *New Scientist*, 12 March 2008.

Gibran, Khalil. *The Prophet*. London: Heinemann, 1964.

Hoff Conow, B. *The Bahá'í Teachings*. Oxford: George Ronald, 1990.

Hofman, David. *The Renewal of Civilization*. Oxford: George Ronald, 1969.

Hooper, Simon. *The Rise of the New Atheists*. CNN, 2006. Available at http://www.cnn.com.

Hornby, H. (comp.). *Lights of Guidance: A Bahá'í Reference File*. New Delhi: Bahá'í Publishing Trust, 5th ed. 1997.

Huntingdon, Samuel. *The Clash of Civilizations and the Remaking of World Order*. London: Simon and Schuster, Touchstone Books, 1997.

Le Poidevin, Robin. *Arguing for Atheism: An Introduction to the Philosophy of Religion*. London: Routledge, 1996.

Libo, Sun. 'Morality, Law and Religion', in Charles O. Lerche (ed.): *Toward the Most Great Justice: Elements of Justice in the New World Order*. London: Bahá'í Publishing Trust, 1996.

Matthews, Gary. *He Cometh With Clouds*. Oxford: George Ronald, 1996.

McLaughlin, Robert. *These Perspicuous Verses*. Oxford: George Ronald, 1982.

Medawar, Jean. *A Very Decided Preference: Life with Peter Medawar*. London: Oxford University Press, 1990.

Phelps, Stephen. Article in *One Country*, March 2007.

Rand, Ayn. *Capitalism: The Unknown Ideal*. New York: Signet, 1967.

Sacherman, J. *Cognitive Processes and the Suppression of Sound Scientific Ideas.* 1997.
Available at: www. amasci.com/supress1.html.

Schaefer, Udo. *Bahá'í Ethics in the Light of Scripture.* 2 vols. Oxford: George Ronald, 2007, 2009.

The Clash of Religions. Zero Palm Press, 1995.

The Imperishable Dominion. Oxford: George Ronald, 1983.

Schaefer, Udo; Towfigh, Nicola; Gollmer, Ulrich. *Making the Crooked Straight: A Contribution to Bahá'í Apologetics.* Oxford: George Ronald, 2000.

Sears, William. *Release the Sun.* Wilmette, IL: Bahá'í Publishing Trust, rev. ed. 1995.

Shaw, George Bernard. *Back to Methusaleh: A Metabiological Pentateuch.* 1921. Available at www.gutenberg.org.

Shoghi Effendi. *The Promised Day Is Come* (1941). Wilmette, IL: Bahá'í Publishing Trust, rev. ed. 1980.

— Summary Statement to the Special UN Committee on Palestine, 1947.

— *The World Order of Bahá'u'lláh: Selected Letters by Shoghi Effendi* (1938). Wilmette, IL: Bahá'í Publishing Trust, 2nd rev. ed. 1974.

Smart, Ninian. *World Philosophies.* London: Routledge, 2000.

Tischler, Elizabeth. *You, Too, Are a Believer!* New York: Vintage Press, 2000.

Townshend, George. *The Heart of the Gospel.* Oxford, George Ronald, 1952.

Toynbee, Arnold. *A Study of History.* 12 vols. Oxford: Oxford University Press, 1938–61.

The Universal House of Justice. *Message to the World's Religious Leaders.* Haifa: Bahá'í World Centre, 2002.

— *The Promise of World Peace.* Haifa: Bahá'í World Centre, 1985.

References

Foreword

1   Quoted in Tischler, *You, Too, Are a Believer!*, pp. 13–14.

1 Is Atheism a Theism?

1   Andrew Brown, in *The Guardian* newspaper, 22 April 2013.

2   'Abdu'l-Bahá, *Selections*, no. 30, p. 61.

3   Schaefer, *The Imperishable Dominion*, p. 167.

4   Dingle, *The Scientific Adventure*, p. 351.

5   Quoted from *Bahá'í Exchange*, 2010.

6   See, for example, Simon Hooper, *The Rise of the New Atheists*.

7   See for example Sacherman, *Cognitive Processes and the Suppression of Sound Scientific Ideas*.

8   Angell, *The New Barbarian Manifesto*, p. 185.

9   Allott, *Eunomia*, p. 94.

10   Bahá'í International Community, *One Common Faith*, p. 46.

11   'Abdu'l-Bahá, *'Abdu'l-Bahá in London*, p. 66.

12   'Abdu'l-Bahá, *The Promulgation of Universal Peace*, p. 29.

13   'Abdu'l-Bahá, ibid. p. 128.

14   Bahá'u'lláh, *Gleanings*, XXVI, p. 62.

15   'Abdu'l-Bahá, *Some Answered Questions*, no. 59, p. 221.

16   Bahá'u'lláh, *Gleanings*, LXXXII, p. 162.

17   'Abdu'l-Bahá, *Some Answered Questions*, no. 51, p. 199.

18   Smart, *World Philosophies*, p. 204.

2 Evolution and Civilization

1   Suheil Bushrui, 'Opening of the Academic Mind', lecture, 2003.

2   Hoff Conow, *The Bahá'í Teachings*, p. 161.

3   Capra, *The Turning Point*, p. 331.

4   ibid. p. 332.
5   Esslemont, *Bahá'u'lláh and the New Era*, pp. 188-9.
6   'Abdu'l-Bahá, *Some Answered Questions,* no. 49, p. 192.
7   'Abdu'l-Bahá, *Abdul Baha on Divine Philosophy*, pp. 89-90.
8   'Abdu'l-Bahá, *The Promulgation of Universal Peace*, p. 369.
9   Interview by Amanda Gefter in *New Scientist*, 12 March 2008.
10 'Abdu'l-Bahá, *Some Answered Questions*, no. 49, pp. 191–94.
11 Cor. 13 :11.
12 Bahá'u'lláh, *Gleanings*, CXI, p. 216.
13 ibid. XIX, pp. 46–7.

3 The Search for Truth

1   Bahá'u'lláh, *Gleanings*, XCV, p. 194.
2   'Abdu'l-Bahá, *The Promulgation of Universal Peace,* pp. 258-9.
3   'Abdu'l-Bahá, *Abdul Baha on Divine Philosophy*, pp. 109-10.
4   Bahá'u'lláh, *Gleanings*, XCIX, p. 200.
5   'Abdu'l-Bahá, *Selections*, no. 159, p. 190.
6   Bahá'u'lláh, *Gleanings*, LXXIV, pp. 141-2.
7   'Abdu'l-Bahá, *Foundations of World Unity*, p.
8   Schaefer, *The Clash of Religions*, p. 135.
9   'Abdu'l-Bahá, *The Promulgation of Universal Peace*, p. 14.
10 Dawkins, *The God Delusion*, p. 305.
11 Gollmer, in Schaefer, Towfigh and Gollmer, *Making the Crooked Straight*, p. 567.
12 Gibran, *The Prophet*, p. 65.
13 Bahá'u'lláh, *Epistle to the Son of the Wolf*, para. 16, p. 13.
14 Sears, *Release the Sun*, p. 206.
15 Bahá'u'lláh, *Gleanings*, XCIII, p. 190.
16 Phelps, article in *One Country*, March 2007.
17 Huntingdon, *The Clash of Civilizations and the Remaking of World Order*, pp. 319–20.
18 Dawkins, *The God Delusion*, p. 168.
19 Matthews, *He Cometh With Clouds*, p. 230.
20 'Abdu'l-Bahá, *The Promulgation of Universal Peace*, pp. 358–9.
21 Darwin, *On the Origin of Species*.
22 'Abdu'l-Bahá, *Some Answered Questions*, no. 2, p. 5.

23 'Abdu'l-Bahá, 'Abdul-Bahá in London, p. 23.
24 Bahá'u'lláh, Epistle to the Son of the Wolf, pp. 26–7.
25 Gail, 'Millennium', in Dawn Over Mount Hira, p. 168.
26 'Abdu'l-Bahá, Selections, no. 143, p. 167.
27 'Abdu'l-Bahá, The Promulgation of Universal Peace, p. 177.
28 Bahá'u'lláh, Short Obligatory Prayer, found in most Bahá'í prayer books.
29 Qur'án 2 :57.
30 Universal Declaration of Human Rights (UDHR), Article 18.
31 Shakespeare, Hamlet, Act V, sc. 2.

4 The Evolution of Spirituality

1 Schaefer, Beyond the Clash of Religions, p. 137.
2 McLaughlin, These Perspicuous Verses, p. 27.
3 Exod. 21: 23–6.
4 Bahá'í International Community. A Bahá'í Declaration of Human Obligations and Rights.
5 Angell, The New Barbarian Manifesto, p. 167.
6 Libo, 'Morality, Law and Religion', p. 68.
7 Dawkins, The God Delusion, p. 167.
8 ibid. p. 419.
9 Professor Francisco Ayala, Templeton Address, 2010.
10 'Abdu'l-Bahá, The Promulgation of Universal Peace, p. 49.
11 'Abdu'l-Bahá, Tablet to Dr. Auguste Henri Forel.
12 Prentice, doctoral thesis.
13 Hofman, The Renewal of Civilization, p. 82.
14 'Abdu'l-Bahá, The Promulgation of Universal Peace, p. 364.
15 ibid. p. 363.
16 Gandhi, Young India, 24 November 1927, p. 393.
17 Matt. 5:18.
18 Bahá'u'lláh, quoted by Shoghi Effendi in The Promised Day Is Come, p. 76.
19 'Abdu'l-Bahá, Selections, no. 19, p. 41.
20 'Abdu'l-Bahá, Abdul Baha on Divine Philosophy, p. 168.
21 'Abdu'l-Bahá, The Promulgation of Universal Peace, p. 225.
22 Bahá'u'lláh, Hidden Words, Arabic no. 66.

5 The Battle for Hearts and Minds

1   Shaw, Preface to *Back to Methusaleh* (1921).
2   Gen. 2:28.
3   'Abdu'l-Bahá, *Some Answered Questions*, no. 22, p. 101.
4   Schaefer, *Making the Crooked Straight*, p. 15.
5   Matthews, *He Cometh With Clouds*, p. 141.
6   Dawkins, *The God Delusion*, p. 246.
7   *New Scientist*, 12 March 2005, p. 33.
8   'Abdu'l-Bahá, *Paris Talks*, no. 7, p. 22.
9   Bahá'u'lláh, Tablet of Aḥmad, in most Bahá'í prayer books.
10 'Abdu'l-Bahá, *The Promulgation of Universal Peace*, p. 143.
11 Dawkins, *The God Delusion*, p. 284.
12 Matt. 5 :18.
13 'Abdu'l-Bahá, *The Promulgation of Universal Peace*, p. 267.
14 'Abdu'l-Bahá, *Abdul Baha on Divine Philosophy*, p. 106.
15 Bahá'í International Community, *Who is Writing the Future?*
16 Shoghi Effendi, Summary Statement to the UN Special Committee on Palestine, 1947.

6 The Purpose of Religion

1   'Abdu'l-Bahá, *Some Answered Questions*, no. 52, pp. 200–01.
2   Jean Medawar, *A Very Distinct Preference: Life with Peter Medawar*.
3   Angell, *The New Barbarian Manifesto*, p. 26.
4   Gollmer, in Schaefer et al., *Making the Crooked Straight*, p. 567.
5   'Abdu'l-Bahá, *Some Answered Questions*, no. 47, p. 184.
6   'Abdu'l-Bahá, *Abdul Baha on Divine Philosophy*, pp. 109–10.
7   Shoghi Effendi, *The Promised Day Is Come*, pp. 112–13.
8   See for example Bahá'u'lláh, *The Kitáb-i-Íqán*, revealed in 1861, for an explanation of this and of the true meanings behind the traditions of Judaism, Christianity and Islám.
9   Bahá'u'lláh, Lawḥ-i-Dunyá, in *Tablets*, p. 87.
10 'Abdu'l-Bahá, *Paris Talks*, ch. 44, p. 150.
11 Phelps, review of *The God Delusion*, in *One Country*, March 2007.
12 The Universal House of Justice, *Message to the World's Religious Leaders*, April 2002.

13   Capra, *The Turning Point,* p. 257.

14   Schaefer, *The Imperishable Dominion*, pp. 79–80.

15   Letter on behalf of Shoghi Effendi to an individual, 19 March 1945, in Hornby (ed.), *Lights of Guidance*, no. 1842.

16   Shakespeare, *Hamlet,* Act 3, sc. 1.

17   Townshend, *Heart of the Gospel,* p. 52.

18   Le Poidevin, *Arguing for Atheism.*

19   ʻAbduʼl-Bahá, Tablet to Dr. Auguste Henri Forel, p. 41.

20   Capra, *The Turning Point*, p. 11.

21   ʻAbduʼl-Bahá, *Abdul Baha in London*, p. 81.

22   ʻAbduʼl-Bahá, *Abdul Baha on Divine Philosophy*, pp. 105–6.

23   ʻAbduʼl-Bahá, *Paris Talks*, no. 5, p. 12.

24   Baháʼuʼlláh, *Gleanings*, XXIX, pp. 71–2.

25   ʻAbduʼl-Bahá, *Some Answered Questions*, no. 22, p. 101.

26   ʻAbduʼl-Bahá, *The Promulgation of Universal Peace, p. 144.*

27   Allott, *Eunomia*, ch. 6, p. 19.

28   Capra, Preface to *The Tao of Physics.*

29   The Universal House of Justice, *The Promise of World Peace*, section I, para. 1.

CPSIA information can be obtained
at www.ICGtesting.com
Printed in the USA
FFOW01n1332260914
7576FF